ACTS OF LIGHT

EMILY DICKINSON

POEMS BY
EMILY DICKINSON

PAINTINGS BY
NANCY EKHOLM BURKERT

APPRECIATION BY
JANE LANGTON

NEW YORK GRAPHIC SOCIETY

BOSTON

The poetry of Emily Dickinson is reprinted from the sources below. The versions chosen for this book are those of the Little, Brown edition.

THE POEMS OF EMILY DICKINSON, edited by Thomas H. Johnson, Cambridge, Mass.: The Belknap Press of Harvard University Press, Copyright © 1951, 1955, 1979 by the President and Fellows of Harvard College. By permission of the publishers and the Trustees of Amherst College.

EMILY DICKINSON FACE TO FACE, by Martha D. Bianchi. Copyright 1932 by Martha Dickinson Bianchi. Copyright © renewed 1960 by Alfred Leete Hampson. By permission of Houghton Mifflin Company.

THE LIFE AND LETTERS OF EMILY DICKINSON, by Martha D. Bianchi. Copyright 1924 by Martha Dickinson Bianchi. Copyright renewed 1952 by Alfred Leete Hampson. By permission of Houghton Mifflin Company.

THE COMPLETE POEMS OF EMILY DICKINSON, edited by Thomas H. Johnson. Copyright © 1914, 1929, 1935, 1942 by Martha Dickinson Bianchi; Copyright © 1957, 1963 by Mary L. Hampson. By permission of Little, Brown and Company.

Edited by Robin Bledsoe
Copyedited by Betsy Pitha
Designed by Lance Hidy
Production coordinated by Nan Jernigan
Typeset in Dante (text) and Centaur (display)
by Michael & Winifred Bixler
Printed by Princeton Polychrome Press
Color separations by Offset Separations
Text paper (Mohawk Superfine) supplied by
Mohawk Paper Mills; insert paper (LOE Dull)
supplied by S. D. Warren Paper Company
Bound by A. Horowitz and Son

New York Graphic Society books are published by Little, Brown and Company. Published simultaneously in Canada by Little, Brown and Company (Canada) Limited.

First Edition   Printed in the United States of America

ISBN 0-8212-1098-X   ISBN 0-8212-1118-8 (deluxe edition)   80-19848

CONTENTS

I dwell in Possibility—
A fairer House than Prose—
More numerous of Windows—
Superior—for Doors—

Of Chambers as the Cedars—
Impregnable of Eye—
And for an Everlasting Roof
The Gambrels of the Sky—

Of Visitors—the fairest—
For Occupation—This—
The spreading wide my narrow Hands
To gather Paradise—

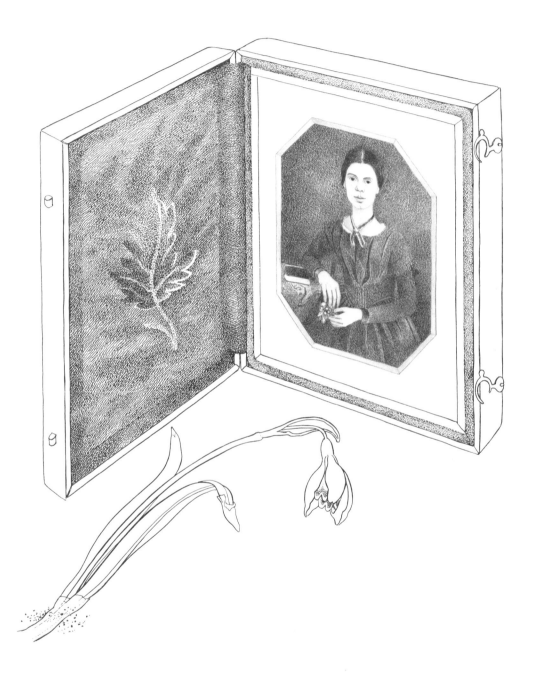

EMILY DICKINSON

AN APPRECIATION

THE FIRE

> Just after we passed Mr Clapps — it thundered more & the thunder &
> lightning increased — [Emily] called it *the fire* — the time the rain wind &
> darkness came we were along in those pine woods — the thunder echoed —
> I will confess that I felt rather bad . . . the horse when the rain came with
> such fury shook his head & galloped on.

"The fire" — in a letter written by her Aunt Lavinia we hear the first recorded words of
the child who was to become the poet Emily Dickinson. On December 10, 1830, two
years before this stormy journey, she had been born in a house built by her grand-
father in the town of Amherst. It was the same house in which she would one day die,
after spending nearly all her life in this single village in western Massachusetts.

OH A VERY GREAT TOWN IS THIS!

Nineteenth-century Amherst was a farming center and a college town. Conservative
in politics and religion, it was many miles west of more liberal Boston and Cambridge.
But it was more than a sleepy backwater. Mrs. Elizabeth Hannum writes proudly of

its busy public life in one of her lively letters: ". . . there is something a going on in Amherst almost all of the time such as Shows Conserts Uncle Toms Calbin performed Musters Festivals Fairs Liceums Exebitions Letures Commencements and Cattle Shows."

The Amherst of festivals and fairs and cattle shows was the town from which the mature poet would at last withdraw, to turn her attention to a different kind of goings-on:

> The Only News I know
> Is Bulletins all Day
> From Immortality.
>
> The Only Shows I see —
> Tomorrow and Today —
> Perchance Eternity —

But in Emily Dickinson's girlhood there was no shrinking away from the life of the town. Her movements were no more restricted than those of the other young women of her circle. Like them she probably attended a local primary school as a small child, and at nine she began going eagerly every day to Amherst Academy. Her grandfather had been one of the founders of the academy, and of Amherst College. In his opinion, "Daughters should be *well instructed.* . . . The female mind, so sensitive, so susceptible of improvement should not be neglected. . . . God hath designed nothing in vain."

Amherst Academy was a remarkable institution. Orthodox Congregational religious instruction was only part of a curriculum that was especially strong in the sciences. "We have a very fine school. . . . I have four studies. They are Mental Philosophy, Geology, Latin, and Botany. How large they sound, don't they?" In the same letter fourteen-year-old Emily boasts jokingly, "I am growing handsome very fast indeed! I expect I shall be the belle of Amherst when I reach my 17th year."

But three years later Emily was to spend her seventeenth year studying in neighboring South Hadley at Mount Holyoke Female Seminary. Here too a heavy padding of religious dogma was stuffed into all the cracks of each day's instruction, and once again there was a solid grounding in the sciences, with lectures in chemistry, electricity, physiology, botany, algebra, Euclid. There was hardly time to be a belle. "At 6. oclock we all rise. We breakfast at 7. Our study hours begin at 8. At 9. we all meet in Seminary Hall, for devotions. At 10¼. I recite a review of Ancient History. . . . We have

Supper at 6. & silent-study hours from then until the retiring bell, which rings at 8¾ . . . ."

Emily stayed at Mount Holyoke only a year. At eighteen, she was back in Amherst for good, enjoying a brisk social life with her younger sister, Lavinia, and the friends of her girlhood and with young men from her father's law office and the college.

Candy Pulling!!
Mr Gould will be happy
to see Miss Dickinson at Miss
Montagues this evening at 6 o clock.

Sometimes there was almost too much to do, especially during college vacations when older brother Austin was free to take part in the "general uproar."

> . . . Amherst is alive with fun this winter—might you be here to see! Sleigh rides are as plenty as people. . . . Parties cant find fun enough—because all the best ones are engaged to attend balls a week beforehand—beaus can be had for the taking—maids smile like the mornings in June—Oh a very great town is this!

There were affairs of the heart—

> . . . While I washed the dishes at noon in that little 'sink-room' of our's, I heard a well-known rap, and a friend I love *so* dearly came and asked me to ride in the woods, the sweet-still woods, and I wanted to exceedingly—I told him I could not go, and he said he was disappointed—he wanted me very much. . . .

There were secrets and excitements—

> I am confided in by one—and *despised* by an *other*! and another still!

But Emily's social life was more than sleighing parties and levees and rides with sophomores. Her father was a prominent citizen of Amherst and treasurer of the college, and thus his three children were close to all the larger events of the town. "Our house is crowded daily with the members of this world," wrote Emily, "the high and the low, the bond and the free, the 'poor in this world's goods,' and the 'almighty dollar' . . ." Every year Mr. Dickinson played host at a splendid Commencement tea, for which there must have been a bustle of preparation beforehand by the women of the family—Mrs. Dickinson, Emily, Lavinia, and the kitchen help behind the scenes (like Margaret O'Brien and later the staunch and formidable Maggie Maher). When Emily was fifteen she climbed to the top of the State House in Boston, after her father was elected to the Massachusetts state legislature. When she was twenty-four she went all the way to Washington with Lavinia to see him as a one-term Whig member of Congress, and stopped off in Philadelphia on the way home.

Back in Amherst few public events could take place without Edward Dickinson on the platform, to address the Temperance Festival and Cold Water Army, to speak in Town Meeting against the sale of intoxicating drinks, to lay the cornerstone of a new college building, to raise the bounty for Union volunteers, to call for subscriptions to the American Telegraph Company, to preside at a "grand Republican rally" at the election of President Grant, or to raise shares for the Amherst & Belchertown Rail Road, which soon brought "the cars" almost to his very door. In 1853 Emily was

Edw Dickinson Amherst

4

amused by the sight of her father leading a parade of the first railroad passengers from New London. "Father was as usual, Chief Marshal of the day, and went marching around the town with New London at his heels like some old Roman General. . . ."

Edward Dickinson's ambitions may have been stiffened by his own father's financial failure. The elder Dickinson had been generous but improvident in his devotion to the new college, and in 1833 he lost the family homestead on Main Street and moved to Cincinnati. His married son stayed on in the house with his wife and three small children, renting half of it from the new owner. Edward was determined to improve his lot: ". . . nothing human shall stop me from making one desperate attempt to make my fortune . . . half a house, & a rod square for a garden, won't answer my turn. . . . I am in earnest." Diligently he applied himself to his college duties, his legal practice, and other affairs. "I like," he said, "the battle of business."

By the time Emily was nine years old, her father's financial condition had improved. He bought a house of his own on Pleasant Street. Fifteen years later his success was so complete that he was able to regain possession of the Main Street homestead, and in 1855 the family moved back into the house in which all of the children had been born. For Edward Dickinson it must have been a moment of triumph. The wonder of the neighbors shows in another of Mrs. Hannum's letters: ". . . it Cost him I understood over five thousands to repair it it is a Splendid House and every thing about the House is the same. . . ."

Edward Dickinson was a complicated man. His heart, said Emily, was "vast." It was "pure and terrible." She regarded him with an awe mixed with comic appreciation for his old-fashioned dignity: "Father steps like Cromwell when he gets the kindlings." Clashes of will with his obedient daughter were few, but Emily could be stubborn too: "Oh! dear!" wrote Lavinia, "Father is killing the horse. . . . Emilie is screaming to the top of her voice." But sometimes in Emily's letters we can hear him laugh, and when he rang the church bell to alert his fellow townsmen to a display of the northern lights, Edward Dickinson seems not ill-suited to be the father of a poet.

By 1855 when he brought his family back to the Homestead his three children had grown up. Austin was twenty-six, Emily twenty-four, Lavina twenty-two. As a family of adults they remained close-knit and intensely loyal. Letters from traveling Dickinsons often sounded homesick. Austin had been as far away as Boston to teach school after graduating from Amherst, and then he had spent a year in Cambridge at Harvard Law School. But now he was at home again to join his father's law practice, and soon he would marry Emily's girlhood friend Susan Gilbert and move three hundred feet away into a fine new house next door. Eventually he was to succeed his father as treasurer of the college. But Austin was not another Edward Dickinson. In the immediate family he was closest to Emily, sharing her joyous response to nature, her wit, her fervent sensibility, her vulnerability to mental suffering.

At first glance younger sister Lavinia seems made of different stuff. Emily said of her, "if we had come up for the first time from two wells . . . her astonishment would not be greater at some things I say." Vinnie was more sturdy and practical, and she willingly left intellectual undertakings to her sister: Emily "had to think—she was the only one of us who had that to do." But Vinnie too was clever, with a sense of fun that turned sharp as she grew older. She was crucial to Emily, who confessed, "I feel the oddest fright at parting with her for an hour, lest a storm arise, and I go unsheltered."

The only member of the family who has left a shadowy imprint on history is Emily's mother, Emily Norcross Dickinson. One suspects she was the kind of person of whom Emily wondered, "How do most people live without any thoughts?" Often ill with nameless complaints, Mrs. Edward Dickinson seems to have been a simple person, living for her family, her house, her garden. Probably she was more important to her daughter than the scant records show, providing Emily with maternal affection and domestic instruction, and creating for her the embracing comfort of an attractive home.

That home still stands on the north side of Main Street, next door to Austin's. The two houses rise high over the road, large and spacious, half-hidden behind evergreens.

It is easy to understand Emily's devotion to the Homestead, to her conservatory, her sunny upstairs room, the garden that sloped gently downhill to the east, and the orchard where "the noiseless noise" was. Home was so agreeable, why would anyone want to go away?

But when she moved back to it in 1855 from the house on Pleasant Street, Emily had not yet adopted a life of seclusion behind the latch of a single garden gate. She and Vinnie settled down into the life of unmarried women in their father's house. The youthful sociability of sugaring parties and rides in the woods was over, and most of their women friends were married. The young college students who had been their contemporaries had graduated and gone away. But the busy town beyond the front door of the Homestead still claimed for a few years longer the presence of Edward Dickinson's elder daughter.

Something was "a going on in Amherst almost all of the time." The noisiest annual event was the Cattle Show. In 1851 the Butter and Cheese Committee included Emily's mother, in 1855 Vinnie served on the Committee for Fine Arts and Fancy Articles, in 1856 Austin judged carriage horses in pairs and Emily won second prize for her rye-and-Indian bread, in 1867 Edward Dickinson drove a "very showy black horse" in the morning cavalcade. The local paper, *The Amherst Express*, kept track of all the Cattle Show doings, and it followed the rest of the town's news—the conflagration in the hat factory, the burning of Cutler's Block, where the Dickinsons had once bought lamp chimneys, kerosene, corsets, and bars of soap. There was scandalous news too, but that was left to the gossips. One visitor complained that it was "one large part of the business of that village to tell of the *wicked doings* of men." There was the crazy woman in the church to talk about, the excommunication for child abuse, the hasty marriage, the man tarred and ridden out of town on a rail.

With the coming of the railroad the town's horizons grew broader. The world came to Amherst on the cars, unloading at the depot on Main Street. Many an arriving procession passed Squire Dickinson's house, including Van Amburgh's New Great Golden Menagerie and G. F. Bailey's Great Quadruple Combination. "Friday I tasted life," wrote Emily. "It was a vast morsel. A circus passed the house—still I feel the red in my mind."

The train brought lecturers to the lyceums: Wendell Phillips, Richard Henry Dana, Horace Greeley, Charles Sumner, Thomas Wentworth Higginson. When Ralph Waldo Emerson spent the night next door, Austin's wife, Sue, said it was like "meeting a God face to face." The railroad brought the daily *Springfield Republican*, edited by

Austin's friend Samuel Bowles. It brought literary magazines from Boston and New York. It carried books to Adams's bookstore, to the college library, to all the Dickinsons—novels by Charles Dickens and George Eliot, the poems of Elizabeth Barrett Browning, Emerson's *Essays*, Thoreau's *Walden*. Streams of books flowed through the two households. Emily and Sue exchanged favorites. Edward bought books for his daughter, although she complained that he begged her not to read them, because he feared "they joggle the Mind." But her father was not as straitlaced as the professors at Amherst Academy who would not teach Shakespeare. In 1857 he bought an eight-volume set of Shakespeare's plays.

The river of books was Emily Dickinson's lifeblood. The authors were her heroes and heroines:

> Strong Draughts of Their Refreshing Minds
> To drink – enables Mine
> Through Desert or the Wilderness
> As bore it Sealed Wine –
>
> To go elastic . . .

Was that what Amherst was to her, a desert, a wilderness? Sometimes it was surely the best grist for her mill – like the circus, a taste of life:

> Menagerie to me
> My Neighbor be –

And often she relished what she saw with avid delight: "I know of no choicer ecstasy than to see Mrs [Luke Sweetser] roll out in crape every morning, I suppose to intimidate antichrist. . . ."

In the end she put it all behind her. Emily Dickinson began her slow withdrawal by avoiding the sewing societies, where, she said, "I am already set down as one of those brands almost consumed." She finished by retiring completely to the Homestead, to the small circle of mother, father, and sister Lavinia. Two distressing absences from home in 1864 and 1865 may have bolstered her determination never to leave again. A mysterious eye complaint required her to spend many months with her Norcross cousins in Cambridgeport while undergoing treatment by a Boston ophthalmologist, who forbade her even the solace of reading. (When the restriction was removed, she "devoured the luscious passages" in her Shakespeare. ("I thought I should tear the leaves out as I turned them.")

These therapeutic journeys were the last of her travels. By the time she was in her late thirties Emily Dickinson's seclusion was complete. "I do not cross my Father's ground to any House or town." Then in 1874 death claimed the father who had been so large a figure in her life, who owned the "ground." Her family was reduced to sister Vinnie and their invalid mother, supported by faithful domestic servants like Maggie Maher and Thomas Kelley. Even the path to Austin's was long since unfamiliar to Emily. With the exception of one harrowing night in 1883 when her little nephew Gilbert lay dying, she did not enter the house next door. And only the choicest friends were welcomed at home. Her connection with the world at large was conducted entirely by correspondence—a paper link that was not necessarily a fragile one. Writing letters was as natural to Emily Dickinson as breathing. Often her notes were accompanied by flowers, by poems, by gifts of her own cooking. Her isolation was physical. It was restricted in space. No longer did she present herself in person beyond the limits of her house and garden.

But the poet in Emily Dickinson had seen enough of the town that lay beyond. The rural village of her birth had not been barren soil. In these lines she may have been thinking of her native Amherst:

> Soil of Flint, if steady tilled–
> Will refund the Hand–

One part of Amherst life that could not be put away as easily as the gossip of the sewing societies was the Congregational church. Every day the bell rang at noon, a reminder that God had measured off another milestone toward the Second Coming. The First Church of Christ was an inheritor of Jonathan Edwards's Great Awakening, of Connecticut Valley Calvinist tradition. The college too was denominational, scorned by Unitarian Harvard as a "priest factory." Many revivals swept the town during Emily Dickinson's lifetime. The call to which all were summoned was the blessed state called conversion. Church membership was not a birthright. It was earned only by an extraordinary spiritual transformation. To young Emily, conversion made "the faces of good men shine, and bright halos come around them; and the eyes of the disobedient look down, and become ashamed."

The Dickinsons were churchgoers (twice on Sunday), but they were not pushovers for conversion. Emily's father was forty-seven years old before he was persuaded. "His pastor said to him . . . 'You want to come to Christ as a *lawyer*—but you must come to him as a *poor sinner*—get down on your knees & let me pray for you. . . .'" His son, Austin, was admitted to the church "by profession" a few months before his marriage at twenty-seven. Daughter Vinnie was an easier mark. At seventeen she wrote her brother from Ipswich Female Seminary, "Oh! Austin . . . How beautiful, if *we three* could all believe in Christ. . . . Does Emilie think of these things at all? Oh! that she might!"

Emily thought of them, often and profoundly, but she did not give in. It is impossible now to imagine the pressure against which she stood fast, the power and influence ranged against her in a town like Amherst, where the church loomed so large, where the clergyman was a man of supreme importance, where sermons were a matter of daily comment. As a dutiful daughter Emily went to church and sat in one of the family pews. But, although she was often moved by the sermons, there were Sundays, even later in life, when she refused to go: "They hunted high and low, & went to church without her. . . . Some hours after, Emily was discovered calmly rocking in a chair placed in the cellar bulk-head, where she had made old Margaret lock her in. . . ."

At Mount Holyoke the pressure mounted. The students were sorted into those "with hope" and those "without," and the hopeless ones were prayed over and exhorted. Even the mortal illness of a young woman at the seminary became part of the pressure, as recorded in the Mount Holyoke Journal: "Our sick one still lingers with us. . . . Her greatest desire this morning is, to persuade her impenitent friends to flee to Christ."

The loving earnestness of her teachers deeply affected Emily Dickinson, but she held her ground. A story about her stubborn independence sounds true: "Miss Lyon . . . asked all those who wanted to be Christians to rise. The wording of the request was not such as Emily could honestly accede to and she remained seated—the only one who did not rise. . . . she said, 'They thought it queer I didn't rise. . . . I thought a lie would be queerer.'"

It wasn't easy to be one of the impenitent. "I regret that last term, when that golden opportunity was mine, that I did not give up and become a Christian. It is not now too late . . . but it is hard for me to give up the world."

She was never to give it up. Emily Dickinson remained the only one in her family who did not become a church member.

What was "the world" she refused to abandon? What world did she mean? It was certainly not Melville's round globe of far-ranging ships and foreign oceans, nor the cosmopolitan literary world of the man who was to become her mentor, Thomas Wentworth Higginson. It was not even Henry Thoreau's tramping exploration of a single town. And yet, Emily Dickinson's world was a very large place indeed—a house, a few acres of ground, and a spreading cone of vision that looked outward and upward infinitely far.

THE EARTH AND I, ALONE

Were the country landscapes of New England in the nineteenth century, their trees and fields and skies, more beautiful than the scenery of other places and other times? Perhaps it was only that the eyes of some New Englanders were more sensitive. "Give me the obscure life," said Henry Thoreau, ". . . the smallest share of all things but poetic perception. Give me but the eyes to see the things which you possess."

Looking around her at blazing August noons, at the sun rising over the Pelham Hills, at the wind moving in her father's trees, Emily Dickinson too knew the importance of perceiving. "Revelation" did not have to be put off till Judgment Day. Revelation was perception. One had only to open one's eyes here and now:

> Not "Revelation"–'tis–that waits,
> But our unfurnished eyes–

Her eyes were "furnished." They saw and perceived. And she was thereby converted, not to the church, but to the spell that nature laid upon her.

> I think I was enchanted
> When first a sombre Girl—
> I read that Foreign Lady—
> The Dark—felt beautiful—
>
> And whether it was noon at night—
> Or only Heaven—at Noon—
> For very Lunacy of Light
> I had not power to tell—
>
> . . .
>
> The Days—to Mighty Metres stept—
> The Homeliest—adorned
> As if unto a Jubilee
> 'Twere suddenly confirmed—
>
> I could not have defined the change—
> Conversion of the Mind
> Like Sanctifying in the Soul—
> Is witnessed—not explained—
>
> 'Twas a Divine Insanity—
> The Danger to be Sane
> Should I again experience—
> 'Tis Antidote to turn—
>
> To Tomes of solid Witchcraft—
> Magicians be asleep—
> But Magic—hath an Element
> Like Deity—to keep—

It was an insanity more precious than sanity, a "Lunacy of Light," a changed state like conversion. Over and over again in her poems it was a condition called ecstasy, transport, rapture, even intoxication—

I taste a liquor never brewed—
From Tankards scooped in Pearl—
Not all the Vats upon the Rhine
Yield such an Alcohol!

Inebriate of Air—am I—
And Debauchee of Dew—
Reeling—thro endless summer days—
From inns of Molten Blue—

Emily Dickinson wasn't the only plain-living New Englander to get drunk on nature, hundred-proof, taken straight. Sixty miles away in the town of Concord, Henry Thoreau drank from the same cup:

To have such sweet impressions made on us, such ecstasies begotten of the breezes! . . . There comes into my mind such an indescribable, infinite, all-

absorbing, divine, heavenly pleasure, a sense of elevation and expansion.…
I was daily intoxicated, and yet no man could call me intemperate.

Thoreau was often surprised to find himself alone in his intoxication, to discover that Concord's sturdy farmers were still sober. He alone was "self-appointed inspector of snow storms and rain storms," going about his business early: "It is true, I never assisted the sun materially in his rising, but, doubt not, it was of the last importance only to be present at it."

Like Thoreau, Emily Dickinson felt the importance of her solitary witness. "Nature," she said, "… plays without a friend."

> The Sun went down—no Man looked on—
> The Earth and I, alone,
> Were present at the Majesty—

This rural New England rapture in the majesty of earth and sky had literary consequences. In Concord Thoreau filled his journals with consummate prose descriptions of his daily journeys around Fair Haven Bay or Walden or Flint's Pond. In Amherst Emily Dickinson cast into miraculous poetic set-pieces a whole ornithology of birds, an entomology of bees and butterflies, a spectacular collection of sunsets, a seasonal round of the year.

> We like March—his shoes are Purple.
> He is new and high—
> Makes he Mud for Dog and Peddler—
> Makes he Forests dry—
> Knows the Adder's Tongue his coming
> And begets her spot—
> Stands the Sun so close and mighty—
> That our Minds are hot.
> News is he of all the others—
> Bold it were to die
> With the Blue Birds buccaneering
> On his British sky—

But her artistic use of the nature that lay around her was more than this dazzling fragmentary portraiture of season or robin or wind or bee. It was a transcription of nature's mystery as well. "Nature," she said, "is a Haunted House." As urgently and lovingly as Thoreau, as grandly as Emerson, she tried to capture its transcendental meaning. What *did* it mean, after all? Who was the haunter of nature's house? What was the tremendous significance of each individual perception of tree or bird or sun or sky?

Her answer was not set down in philosophical terms and axioms. She said, "I do not respect 'doctrines.'" Nature's conversion was "witnessed—not explained." Like the transcendentalists she claimed the arrogant right of simple intuition:

> You'll know it–as you know 'tis Noon–
> By Glory–
> As you do the Sun–
> By Glory–
> As you will in Heaven–
> Know God the Father–and the Son.
>
> By intuition, Mightiest Things
> Assert themselves–and not by terms–
> "I'm Midnight"–need the Midnight say–
> "I'm Sunrise"–Need the Majesty?
>
> Omnipotence–had not a Tongue–
> His lisp–is Lightning–and the Sun–
> His Conversation–with the Sea–
> "How shall you know"?
> Consult your Eye!

Here the "omnipotence" that speaks through nature seems to be God, but often the word "God" seems foreign to the vision. Sometimes the doubtful heaven of God is scorned as superfluous. Earth, after all, is heaven enough.

> The Fact that Earth is Heaven–
> Whether Heaven is Heaven or not

More sublime than the word "God" in Emily Dickinson's vocabulary is the word

"Eternity." Each separate moment of awe before nature is grounded upon the vastness of the everlasting. Beyond the single perception at a particular moment of a particular day lies the eternity of which it is a sign and signal. With each instant of vision she plunges into what is eternal and timeless:

> As if the Sea should part
> And show a further Sea—
> And that—a further—and the Three
> But a presumption be—
>
> Of Periods of Seas—
> Unvisited of Shores—
> Themselves the Verge of Seas to be—
> Eternity—is Those—

Sublimity followed her like a companion:

> No Friend have I that so persists
> As this Eternity.

Often in reading the poetry of Emily Dickinson we have the sense that her upstairs room had no ceiling, that the house itself had no roof but was open to the sky, that house and garden lay on a cosmic frontier. All time and space expand around her. Her basket, she said, held firmaments. Her poems exhale a kind of ethereal breath, blown from "Gamuts of Eternities," from "Meadows of Majesty" and "easy Sweeps of Sky."

In this portrait of a single bird we see her visionary logic:

> Upon his Saddle sprung a Bird
> And crossed a thousand Trees
> Before a Fence without a Fare
> His Fantasy did please
> And then he lifted up his Throat
> And squandered such a Note
> A Universe that overheard
> Is stricken by it yet—

This moment here and now, this bird, this note of his song, is of eternal significance. It will never die. It exists eternally. And, like the universe, the poet herself is stricken. The spell, the intoxication, is upon her. The universe pulses near, nearer than the front gate, nearer than the hat factory down the street. Sometimes it presses so close that it is almost unbearable:

> Beauty crowds me till I die
> Beauty mercy have on me
> But if I expire today
> Let it be in sight of thee—

It isn't hard to understand why the small events of Amherst society should be of little consequence to someone whose eye was focused on eternity's horizon, who was perched "On Twigs of singing—rather high." In Concord, Henry Thoreau had retired to Walden with the same lofty urgency. "Why," he said, "should I feel lonely? is not our planet in the Milky Way?"

Neighbors in the same galaxy, Emily Dickinson and Henry Thoreau observed nature with the same rapt attention. He too wrote verses that are still fresh with the smell of earth and the water of the river. But in one essential way they differ. The difference made her the greater poet—

THE NAME OF IT IS LOVE

After falling in love once or twice in his youth, Henry Thoreau seems to have given it up. "There," he said once, kicking a skunk cabbage, "marriage is like that." The reader of his journals is given only a few hints of his affections: "And now another friendship is ended. . . . The heavens withdraw and arch themselves higher."

Emily Dickinson never gave up on love. Her letters to friends and family are intensely affectionate, and her poems are proof that as a mature woman she fell deeply in love more than once.

Only a few witty Valentine verses remain from the period when beaux could be had for the taking. The flood of her poetry did not begin until she was twenty-seven, reaching a crest four years later in 1862. The poems attributed to that year number one for every day.

The inundation may have been the result of her love for someone she addresses as

"Master" in three famous letters. The Master letters have been assigned by students of her handwriting to the late 1850s and early 1860s. (They exist only in draft form and may never have been sent.)

> Master . . . if I wish with a might I cannot repress—that mine were the Queen's place—the love of the Plantagenet is my only apology—To come nearer than presbyteries—and nearer than the new Coat—that the Tailor made—the prank of the Heart at play on the Heart—in holy Holiday—is forbidden me. . . . Would Daisy disappoint you—no—she would'nt— Sir—it were comfort forever—just to look in your face, while you looked in mine—then I could play in the woods till Dark. . . .

In scores of poems we feel her ardor. With breathless hope she envies "the wealthy Fly, upon His Pane," and wishes to be with the loved one always:

> Forever at His side to walk –
> The smaller of the two!
> Brain of His Brain –
> Blood of His Blood –
> Two lives – One Being – now –

With whom was she in love? Was it with Philadelphia clergyman Charles Wadsworth? Emily may have heard Wadsworth preach when she was in Philadelphia in 1855. Little is known about their friendship beyond the fact that she sometimes secreted letters to him in envelopes addressed to others. He is known to have visited her in Amherst in 1860 and again twenty years later.

Or were the Master letters addressed to her brother's friend Samuel Bowles, editor

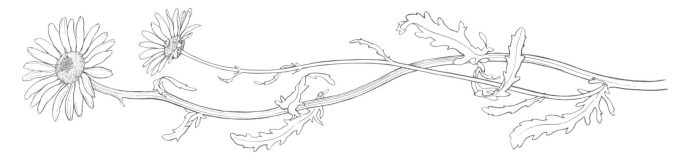

of *The Springfield Republican*? Like Wadsworth, Bowles was a married man
nearer than the new coat the tailor made was forbidden. But some
poems she is known to have sent him betray a passionate
wait until united with him in death.

> Title divine – is mine!
> The Wife – without the Sign!
> Acute Degree – conferred on me –
> Empress of Calvary! . . .
>
>   . . .
>
> "My Husband" – women say –
> Stroking the Melody –
> Is *this* – the way?

Bowles was a man of the world, attractive to women and attracted by them. It is
not known how willing a partner he was in this sacramental contract. Perhaps his
response to this poem was a letter of polite demurral. In another letter probably
written about the same time, Emily seems to draw back into virginal modesty: "If
you doubted my Snow—for a moment—you never will—again."

It is a relief to know that her yearnings were not to go unrequited forever. In her late
forties Emily Dickinson fell in love with Judge Otis Lord of Salem, a widower and a
friend of her late father's. Although they did not marry, her letters to him for the
remaining six years of his life are playful and joyous in a happy sense of mutual delight.

But in the spring of 1862 this long-delayed satisfaction was undreamed of. In a single
month both Wadsworth and Bowles vanished from her horizon—Bowles for a
lengthy trip to Europe, Wadsworth for a pulpit in San Francisco. It was at that very
moment, in the time of her greatest need, that she read in the April issue of *The
Atlantic Monthly* an article by Thomas Wentworth Higginson. His "Letter to a Young
Contributor" was an encouragement to any "mute inglorious Miltons" who might be
readers of the journal.

Afterward Higginson had cause to laugh ruefully at the "wonderful effusions" that
landed on his desk. Among them were four poems by Emily Dickinson and a letter
that began, "Are you too deeply occupied to say if my Verse is alive?" Higginson
wrote back, and it was the beginning of a correspondence that lasted all her life. As an
adviser he failed her. Although he admitted their "strange power," he found her
poems bizarre, and in kindly condescension he urged her not to publish. But at least

he represented a listening ear. In the faraway literary world the poet was no longer unheard. Gratefully she called Higginson her "Preceptor." His letters were, she said, like a hand stretched to her "in the Dark."

How dark the darkness had been, how dark it remained, can be sensed in the desolation of most of her love poems. The consequence of her capacity to love greatly was the equal and opposite capacity to suffer:

> You left me – Sire – two Legacies –
> A Legacy of Love
> A Heavenly Father would suffice
> Had He the offer of –
>
> You left me Boundaries of Pain —
> Capacious as the Sea –
> Between Eternity and Time –
> Your Consciousness – and Me –

Permanent separation from the one she loved was not a temporary disappointment but a lasting anguish. Again and again she inspected her misery, turning it this way and that like a curious object. The pain is harrowing. The words are "blister," "stabbed," "scalds." There are "Gimlets – among the nerve." Sometimes the piercing sharpness gives way to numbness:

> I tie my Hat – I crease my Shawl –
> Life's little duties do – precisely –
> As the very least
> Were infinite – to me –
>
> I put new Blossoms in the Glass –
> And throw the old – away –
> I push a petal from my Gown
> That anchored there – I weigh
> The time 'twill be till six o'clock
> I have so much to do –
> And yet – Existence – some way back –
> Stopped – struck – my ticking – through –

The examination of her suffering is so various, the poems might be catalogued like an encyclopedia. She computes the equation of heartache:

> Limit—how deep a bleeding go!
> So—many—drops—of vital scarlet—
> Deal with the Soul
> As with Algebra!

She calculates its value on the market:

> Sharp pittances of years—
> Bitter contested farthings—
> And Coffers heaped with Tears!

Her poetry has often been examined for signs of the physical hungers and frustrations that might be expected in an unmarried woman who was the daughter of a retiring mother and a powerful father, who lived in a village where the heavy stroke of the Calvinist church bell counted the hours. Of course it would have been as unlikely for Emily Dickinson of Amherst to use explicit sexual language as to fly to the moon, but at least, like the primmest of her contemporaries, she could fall back on the conventional symbolism of the birds and the bees. In this languorous poem the sexual imagery is clear:

> Come slowly—Eden!
> Lips unused to Thee—
> Bashful—sip thy Jessamines—
> As the fainting Bee—
>
> Reaching late his flower,
> Round her chamber hums—
> Counts his nectars—
> Enters—and is lost in Balms.

Unanswered questions remain. Why did Emily never marry? Did she tend to love married men because they were safely unobtainable, because she could not leave the house she so often called "my father's"? Why in her letters and her poetry did she so often adopt the persona of a child? What was the meaning of the white dresses she wore in later life? Were they the color of her virginity, the sign of an unconsummated "marriage"? Why did she not leave home at last to marry Judge Lord? What did she mean by a curious remark in a letter to him: "Dont you know you are happiest while I withhold and not confer—dont you know that 'No' is the wildest word we consign to Language?"

Whatever contemporary interpretations may be placed on these eccentricities, it cannot be denied that Emily Dickinson's feeling could be passionate, and that her heart was well and truly broken by a love that was not returned, or by a profound attachment that ended in separation.

But it was not only the withdrawal of love that tormented her. Death was another kind of sundering. For her, as for everyone, death remorselessly succeeded death. Her father died in 1874, Samuel Bowles in 1878, Charles Wadsworth and her mother in 1882. Then in 1883 death came to the house next door. Austin's and Sue's youngest son

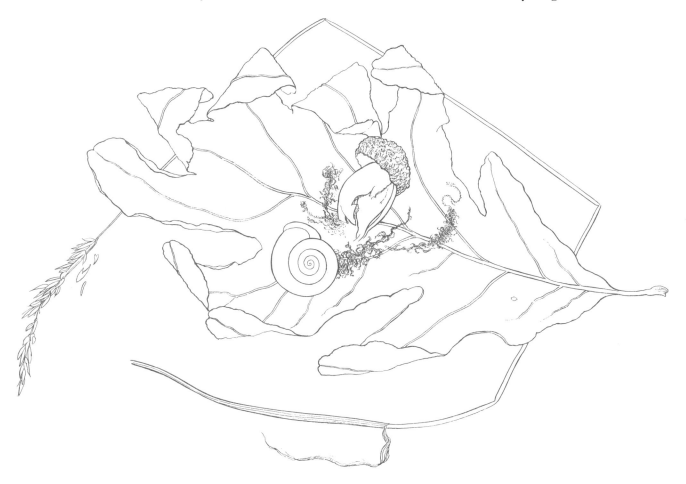

fell ill of "malarial Typhoid" and died suddenly. Eight-year-old Gilbert had been a remarkable child, the darling of the two households. Emily attempted to console her grief-stricken sister-in-law: "I see him in the Star, and meet his sweet velocity in everything that flies." But Emily too was prostrated by this final tragedy, and in another letter she proclaimed the bitter equality of the two things that seemed to fill her world: ". . . *is* there more? More than Love and Death? Then tell me it's name!"

DEATH, WHOSE IF IS EVERLASTING

> They dropped like Flakes—
> They dropped like Stars—
> Like Petals from a Rose—
> When suddenly across the June
> A wind with fingers—goes—

There was a cemetery behind the house on Pleasant Street where Emily Dickinson lived from the time she was nine years old until she was twenty-four. Dickinson graves mounted the hillside, row upon row. Death was a neighbor. Funeral processions were frequent, mortality and resurrection the subjects of a thousand Sunday sermons. For the orthodox, the Christian dualism of an incorruptible soul in a mortal body was a commonplace article of faith. For Emily it was the uneasy foundation stone of her troubled faith, her doubting belief. Could it be true that "A single Screw of Flesh / Is all that pins the Soul"?

Many of her contemporaries put the matter to rest by accepting the certainty of the sermons: "Death is not destruction! . . . Death is harvesting; and the design of the harvest is the preservation of the grain." But for Emily sermons could not "still the Tooth / That nibbles at the soul." The riddle of that "*Bareheaded life*—under the grass" worried her "like a Wasp."

The enigma was central. Emily Dickinson's poems cannot be categorized easily under headings like "Nature," or "Love," or "Loss," but even the feeblest attempt at sorting makes plain her fascination with mortality and the state of existence after death. "You mention Immortality," she wrote Higginson. "That is the Flood subject." With an almost morbid interest she focused her attention on the moment of passage between life and death, eager to capture the fleeting instant when the dying soul would become a party to the secret—forever disappointed, because the dead could not pass on the new discovery: "Once to achieve, annuls the power / Once to communicate–"

"Abyss," she concluded sadly, "has no Biographer." There was no "Affidavit" of heaven.

Once again she turned the subject this way and that, hurling her guesses into the void. Death was a courtly coachman, who "kindly stopped for me." He drove the dead along "that drowsy route / To the surmising Inn." Death was dependable: one could "lean against the Grave." He was "the supple Suitor," the pall was "hospitable," the grave was "cordial." Death was democratic, stopping even for the humblest, yet it conferred the purple majesty of coronation and the crown of immortality, with "Obsequious Angels" and a "royal . . . Retinue."

It was also terrifying. Some of Emily Dickinson's poems convey a shuddering mortuary sense of horror at death's finality. One suspects that the dire Calvinist warnings of Sunday sermons on the subject of perdition were responsible for the fevered poise of a poem like this:

> A Pit – but Heaven over it –
> And Heaven beside, and Heaven abroad,
> And yet a Pit –
> With Heaven over it.
>
> To stir would be to slip –
> To look would be to drop –

Her bad dreams are as eerie as the visions of Poe:

> Escape – it is the Basket
> In which the Heart is caught
> When down some awful Battlement
> The rest of Life is dropt –

It was not the fear of hell-fire that galled her. It was uncertainty. Was there life after death or not? The thought of mere nothingness aroused a dread that quivers in many poems. Again and again she protested against a mystery that seemed malicious. Why should a matter as important as the state of the soul after death be a secret, God's mighty "shall not tell," kept for "a Trillion years"? Everlastingly she balked at "the if of Deity" and at "Death, whose if is everlasting."

MY BUSINESS IS CIRCUMFERENCE

Throughout her life Emily Dickinson was conscious of gaps—between childhood and maturity, girlhood and the "translation" of marriage, the lover and the loved, "no hope" and "hope," the living and the dead, time and eternity. In her poetry there is a perpetual sense of separation, of reaching across an impassable gulf, of crossing a shaking bridge, of hammering at a door that is locked and sealed. One feels that if she could only stretch her hand across the abyss, totter to the other side of the bridge, and fling open the door, then somehow she could unite the two separated things. If only by the main strength of her two fists she could pull them together, then she could achieve her object, "circumference," a rapturous state of suspended fulfillment and perfection.

> She staked her Feathers–Gained an Arc–
> Debated–Rose again–
> This time–beyond the estimate
> Of Envy, or of Men–
>
> And now, among Circumference–
> Her steady Boat be seen–
> At home–among the Billows–As
> The Bough where she was born–

Like a bird she has described a daring arc upon the air, and this time she has completed the circle. She exists at last (whether by exaltation, or by resurrection after death) in a state of bliss called circumference. With the same reverence she uses the word "sum" as another precious totality, in which the random cluttered parts of life, as unlike as apples and oranges, as impossible as an incorruptible soul in a corruptible body, could be added together into a single whole.

But how? How to close the circle, find the sum? In spite of abysses, Alps, doors with "hasps of steel," there was a kind of circumference that was always available to her, one sum that could be achieved at will: the closed circle of a finished poem, the sum of a few perfect stanzas. In the practice of her art there was a kind of seamless perfection like that of the eternal note of the bird's song.

I KEPT IT IN MY HAND – I NEVER PUT IT DOWN

> It was given to me by the Gods –
> When I was a little Girl –

She was a poet. She had been set apart. Her poetry was a gift, a present richer than gold.

> I kept it in my Hand –
> I never put it down –
> I did not dare to eat – or sleep –
> For fear it would be gone –

It was "a reduceless Mine." It was "an Estate perpetual." It was "the Mint / That never ceased to fall." The gift was holy, like "esoteric sips / Of the communion Wine."

The poet exulted in her power. "Every day life feels mightier, and what we have the power to be, more stupendous." Sometimes her confidence was so lofty that she competed with God's own creative power, here in jest —

> I send Two Sunsets –
> Day and I – in competition ran –
> I finished Two – and several Stars –
> While He – was making One –
>
> His own was ampler – but as I
> Was saying to a friend –
> Mine – is the more convenient
> To Carry in the Hand –

and here in arrogant earnest —

I reckon—when I count at all—
First—Poets—Then the Sun—
Then Summer—Then the Heaven of God—
And then—the List is done—

But, looking back—the First so seems
To Comprehend the Whole—
The Others look a needless Show—
So I write—Poets—All—

   It is the proud poet-creator who survives the separations, whose poems reach across the gap to close the circle. In fact, one wonders if the poems would have existed at all if there had been no losses, no groping at impossible barriers, no grief. No one knew better than Emily Dickinson that "A *Wounded* Deer—leaps highest," that anguish was part of the stimulus:

Essential Oils—are wrung—
The Attar from the Rose
Be not expressed by Suns—alone—
It is the gift of Screws—

Dispossession and nagging religious doubt gave an edge to her poetry that no realized satisfaction could have supplied. The bleak endowment of denial kept them at a fever pitch of want and expectation. Abstinence almost became a religion: "'Tis Parching—

vitalizes Wine." The result was poems of a taut and passionate eagerness, accomplished works of art ranging in depth of feeling from terror to rapture in a few bold stanzas. The poet herself complained of the limitation of her compactness: ". . . when I try to organize—my little Force explodes." But force it was. The small compass of her poems was no limit to their power, to the full circle of their circumference and the accumulated total of their tremendous sum.

YOU MUST COME DOWN TO BOSTON SOMETIMES?
ALL LADIES DO.

It was as an artist seeking this kind of rounded perfection that Emily Dickinson withdrew from society. Her solitude was imperative, but to her contemporaries it looked curious and queerly unconventional.

Thomas Wentworth Higginson first encountered it in 1869, when he sent her a bland invitation to hear him speak at the Boston Woman's Club on the Greek goddesses. "You must come down to Boston sometimes? All ladies do."

Emily must have smiled. She issued a counter-invitation, "Could it please your convenience to come so far as Amherst I should be very glad," and wrapped her remoteness about her: "I do not cross my Father's ground to any House or town."

Emily Dickinson was not like "all ladies." Lectures on the goddesses did not interest her. There was too much to do at home, too much of first importance, too much that could not be delayed. Her priorities were like those of Thoreau, who thought it not worth his while to go around the world "to count the cats in Zanzibar," who urged his readers to explore "the private sea, the Atlantic and Pacific Ocean of one's being alone." Emily Dickinson had no need to go to Boston. There were her own interior spaces to examine:

> Soto! Explore thyself!
> Therein thyself shalt find
> The "Undiscovered Continent"
> No Settler had the Mind.

Her chamber was not a refuge of timid hiding, but a pioneering frontier, a place of adventure. Often the floor of that upstairs room became a watery deep on which she was swept out to sea—

Exultation is the going
Of an inland soul to sea,
Past the houses – past the headlands –
Into deep Eternity –

Bred as we, among the mountains,
Can the sailor understand
The divine intoxication
Of the first league out from land?

One day in the grip of this kind of transport she refused to see a caller, sending a note downstairs to explain her need for privacy: "My own Words so chill and burn me." To the visitor it must have seemed a peculiar reason for being turned away. Refusals like this one nourished the myth of the timid wraith who fled from the creak of the gate or the knock at the door. But if the poet was shy of ordinary callers, it was because she had larger company:

Who Giants know, with lesser Men
Are incomplete, and shy –
For Greatness, that is ill at ease
In minor Company –

She was not alone: "Alone, I cannot be – / For Hosts – do visit me –" The impression of withdrawn timidity was only on the surface. Below it, tumultuous forces were at work: "On my volcano grows the Grass." Her quiet was "Earthquake Style." The frightened child who kept to her father's house, who was small as an acorn, was not really small at all—

. . . had you looked in–
A Giant–eye to eye with you, had been–
No Acorn–then–

There was no time to be spared for "lesser Men," for women of "Dimity Convictions," little time even for her old friends, married women now with a domesticated foreignness. In the summer of 1870 Emily was pleased to receive a visit from Higginson in the parlor downstairs, but upstairs at her small desk she did not need even so distinguished a preceptor. She could rely "On a Columnar Self." She stood alone —

The Props assist the House
Until the House is built
And then the Props withdraw
And adequate, erect,
The House support itself
And cease to recollect
The Auger and the Carpenter–
Just such a retrospect
Hath the perfected Life–
A past of Plank and Nail
And slowness–then the Scaffolds drop
Affirming it a Soul.

It should be understood that the grandeur of Emily Dickinson's retirement did not mean perpetual isolation in one room. Emily was the baker of the family bread, the caretaker of her conservatory and of the flowers in the garden, and like Vinnie a nurse to their invalid mother. And of course not everyone was turned away. The children of the neighborhood were especially welcome. One of them published his recollections:

I remember her as slight of stature, quick, graceful and animated in every movement and gesture. I seem to see through the mist of years a mass of glorious auburn hair and a pair of lustrous eyes. These eyes have followed me all my life. They never were the same for a moment, but changing, shifting with her mood. One moment dancing with fun, gleaming with a gentle but defiant wickedness, and melting to a softness and loveliness that filled our hearts with a very new and very wonderful feeling. I recall her as usually dressed in white which added to the effect of fragility and unreality that always baffled me. Baffled me because Miss Emily was not really fragile; she was far too dynamic a person to create any such impression, and she certainly was real. Her participations in our games, her stout defense of us in times of stress, her defiance of Maggie in raiding the pantry that we should be well supplied with cookies or doughnuts, all these were the attributes of a very real and a very human friend and comrade. But it was baffling, for in the midst of her boldest raid in our behalf, a footstep would be heard outside the kitchen door and our laughing goddess of plenty would become the flutter of the edge of a white skirt behind a closing door. . . . She once said to us, as she was busy in the pantry with a group of hungry and expectant youngsters about her: "You know, dears, if the butcher boy should come now, I would jump in the flour barrel."

Among the children to whom Emily Dickinson was a presence rather than an absence was Austin's daughter Matty, who was treated to this vivid explanation of her Aunt Emily's runaway escapes to the privacy of her own room: "She would stand looking down, one hand raised, thumb and forefinger closed on an imaginary key, and say, with a quick turn of her wrist, 'It's just a turn—and freedom, Matty!'"

MY WORDS PUT ALL THEIR FEATHERS ON

In her lifetime Emily Dickinson's poems were generally thought too odd for public print. Odd they remain, but with the singularity of genius. Her distortions of the language are an example of her uniqueness. Her English is her own invention, a curious dialect in which parts of speech are wrenched and forced into outlandish shapes to fit a higher grammar that is hers alone. Adjectives are driven to dizzy extremes: "Admirabler Show," "The Birds jocoser sung." Almost any word can become an exotic negative: "Swerveless Tune," "Perturbless Plan." Words that don't fit are simply omitted:

> How dare I, therefore, stint a faith
> On which so [much that is] vast depends–

And where common usage might call for the declarative mood, Emily Dickinson's poems often riot in a rampaging, giddy, transubstantiated subjunctive:

> Without the Snow's Tableau
> Winter, were lie–to me–
> Because I see–New Englandly–

We can see the method in her skewed syntax in a poem about the sound of the wind:

> Inheritance, it is, to us—
> Beyond the Art to Earn—
> Beyond the trait to take away
> By Robber, since the Gain
> Is gotten not of fingers—
> And inner than the Bone—

The simple adjective "inner" has been pushed into a corner where, by the lucky accident that it happens to end in "er," it seems to mean "more inner," like a comparative. Thus her use of "than" has a bizarre correctness. The phrase succeeds and the reader feels a twinge in the marrow.

Her meter too is distinctive. At first glance it looks simple. Over and over again, three and four beats alternate in four-line quatrains:

> This is my letter to the World
> That never wrote to Me—
> The simple News that Nature told—
> With tender Majesty

In many poems two lines of three beats are followed by a line of four beats and a final line of three:

> I stepped from Plank to Plank
> A slow and cautious way
> The Stars about my Head I felt
> About my Feet the Sea.

These homely rhythms have been traced to the meters of the hymns Emily Dickinson must have sung in church, hymns like this one by Isaac Watts:

> Come, sound his Praise abroad,
> And hymns of Glory sing:
> Jehovah is the Sovereign God,
> The universal King.

She may also have studied hymn meters more carefully in her father's copy of Watts's *Christian Psalmody*. But Emily Dickinson was too original to be content for long with anyone else's rules. Sometimes she took daring liberties with the pat rhythms of the hymns, breaking the singsong meters to suit her meaning:

> Just lost, when I was saved!
> Just felt the world go by!
> Just girt me for the onset with Eternity,
> When breath blew back,
> And on the other side
> I heard recede the disappointed tide!

To Thomas Wentworth Higginson this sort of dramatic irregularity was "uncontrolled," and he reproved her "spasmodic" gait. Nor was he the only one to be put off by her lopsided rhythms and bold ways with rhyme, by lines that matched "pearl" with "bowl," "blood" with "dead," "plucking" with "morning." In her lifetime only a handful of poems by Emily Dickinson was published (all anonymously), although the newspapers and popular journals of her day regularly printed hosts of sentimental verses by less talented women. Perhaps it was because Lizzie Lincoln and Fanny Fern and Grace Greenwood and Minnie Myrtle could be trusted to make pretty twins of all their rhymes and jingle their meters more dependably. Even so august a poet as Oliver Wendell Holmes was grateful to the friend who altered his rhyming at the last minute before going to press, changing his careless matching of "gone" with "forlorn" to a tidier "gone" and "wan."

Reading the doggerel that appeared day after day, year in and year out, in the newspaper edited by Samuel Bowles, Emily must have wondered at it. Jokingly she complained to Higginson of being "the only Kangaroo among the Beauty, Sir."

She was not to be a beauty to Higginson until after her death. His lack of perception has been explained by Dickinson scholar Thomas Johnson: "He was trying to measure a cube by the rules of plane geometry."

THAT PORTION OF THE VISION

Emily Dickinson was amused when her little nephew made a joke: "Ned tells that the Clock purrs and the Kitten ticks." She said he had inherited her own "ardor for the lie." She was talking of course about her fondness for metaphor, the most useful tool in any poet's bag of tricks—lies like these in another poem about the wind:

> On a strange Mob of panting Trees
> And Fences fled away
> And Rivers where the Houses ran
> Those looked that lived–that Day–
> The Bell within the steeple wild
> The flying tidings told–
> How much can come
> And much can go,
> And yet abide the World!

Trees do not pant, fences do not flee, houses do not run, steeples are not wild. But all these shifts and transferences make brilliant images. The fresh breeze that rushes through this poem seems to toss words before it and blow them jumbled in our faces.

More distinctive than "the lie" in the poetry of Emily Dickinson is her use of extraordinary combinations of words. Often she plucks commonplace things from the streets and houses of Amherst and sets them down beside regal abstractions or celestial bodies: "Bring me the sunset in a cup"; "in Sovereign Barns"; "Baronial Bees"; "The Wind . . . Upholsterer - of the Pond"; "The Sunshine threw his Hat away"; "Death . . . His pallid Furniture"; "Eternity's vast pocket, picked"; "Summer folds her miracle - / As Women - do - their Gown." Occasionally the combination is too out-rageous ("That Whiffletree of Amethyst"), but usually her unexpected combinations have a stunning effectiveness:

> The Auctioneer of Parting
> His "Going, going, gone"
> Shouts even from the Crucifix,
> And brings his Hammer down -

Here the grotesque union of the crass word "Auctioneer" with the crucifixion, the sublime pinnacle of pain, is so jolting that we feel a thrill of horror, and the hammer slams down with excruciating force. Our sense of shock is like Emily Dickinson's own definition of poetry: "If I read a book and it makes my whole body so cold no fire ever can warm me I know *that* is poetry. If I feel physically as if the top of my head were taken off, I know *that* is poetry. These are the only ways I know of."

Word pairings are her trademark. Often they are sumptuous combinations of multiple reverberating syllables: "rumor of Delirium"; "Death's tremendous near-ness"; "Purple Ribaldry"; "Edifice of Ocean"; "confiscated Gods." Some of the most sombre and resounding are saved for last lines that are like blows on a gong. A poem that begins as a clever portrait of the rat—

> The Rat is the concisest Tenant.
> He pays no Rent.

—ends by showing his kinship with universal forces of nature:

> Neither Decree prohibit him -
> Lawful as Equilibrium.

Emily Dickinson used a number of special vocabularies. The most majestic words are drawn from the Bible and from the cosmic immensities of theology. Words like "creation," "sacrament," "dominion," "omnipotence," "justified," "resurrection," "judgment," "Calvary" are talismans for her. They roll grandly in her poems with novel meaning to suit her own personal unorthodoxy. In her solemn verbal pageantry the old words are not merely stately Calvinist abstractions but volumes of glowing air:

> My faith that Dark adores–
> Which from its solemn abbeys
> Such resurrection pours.

Other sonorous vocabularies turn up in countless poems. There is a parade of faraway romantic words, of kings and queens, czars and emperors, crowns and diadems. The dusty paraphernalia of castles and courts littered nineteenth-century romantic poetry, but in Emily Dickinson's usage it glitters freshly, like these royal robes belonging to the sun:

> Meanwhile–Her wheeling King–
> Trailed–slow–along the Orchards–
> His *haughty–spangled* Hems–

A great many poems use an idiom that is uniquely Emily Dickinson's own. From her family of lawyers she borrowed scores of dry legal and business terms. Again the combinations are startling: "receipted bliss"; "Codicil of Doubt"; "Indemnity for Loneliness"; "Accquitted–from that Naked Bar–/ Jehovah's Countenance."

But the most surprising words are scientific, drawn from lectures at Amherst Academy and Mount Holyoke. A strangely transfigured mathematics turns up in "the Cube of the Rainbow" and "Exponent of Earth"; geology in "strata of Iniquity"; astronomy in "Enchantment's Perihelion"; and the optics of lenses in "Convex–and Concave Witness." Perhaps she was recollecting a demonstration of electrostatics in the following stanza, and in other lines in which electricity and flashes of lightning stand for the stroke of artistic revelation (the amateur psychologist remembers her journey in the thunderstorm when she was two years old):

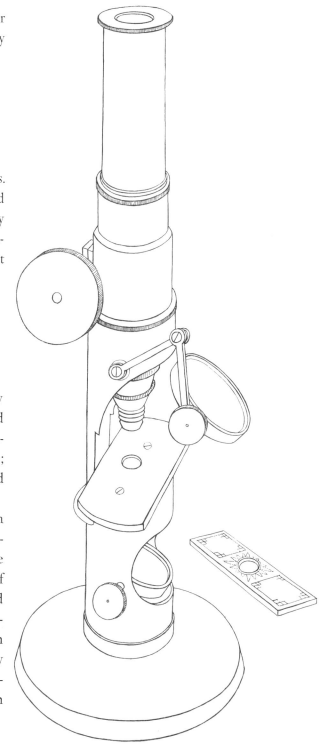

What respite from her thrilling toil
Did Beauty ever take –
But Work might be electric Rest
To those that Magic make –

In one extraordinary poem we seem to see the poet sitting in her bedroom at the very small table that was her desk, choosing among words in her lexicon. The quest for the right word is so important that it will be hailed like a bridegroom. As the poem begins, she seems about to reveal the secret of her method:

Shall I take thee, the Poet said
To the propounded word?
Be stationed with the Candidates
Till I have finer tried –

The Poet searched Philology
And when about to ring
For the suspended Candidate
There came unsummoned in –

That portion of the Vision
The Word applied to fill
Not unto nomination
The Cherubim reveal –

A poem is a vision, not a method. For those on friendly terms with cherubim, riffling through dictionaries is not always necessary.

WHEREFORE SING . . . SINCE NOBODY HEARS?

I found a bird, this morning, down—down—on a little bush at the foot of the garden, and wherefore sing, I said, since nobody *hears*?
    One sob in the throat, one flutter of bosom—"*My* business is to *sing*"—and away she rose!

Emily Dickinson's poems were in constant circulation among her family and friends. She sent them flying from her desk in notes to neighbors, to the house next door, in letters carried by railroad to acquaintances and relatives far away. Every occasion of celebration brought a poem of congratulation from Emily, every grief-stricken household had its verses of sympathy. Poetry was her natural speech, and she took her calling as poet with intense seriousness. But over and over again she must have faced the truth that others did not. The pathos of the passage about the bird that sings unheard is a rare confession of regret at the deafness of the world. Gently discouraged by Higginson and continually overlooked as a poet by the influential editors who were the close friends of her family, she comforted herself with the lofty necessity of her lonely music. Her "business" was to sing.

But there was at least one appreciative listener outside her local circle, the famous novelist Helen Hunt Jackson. During Emily Dickinson's lifetime, "H. H." was almost alone in recognizing her genius. Again and again she asked for Emily's poems and urged her to publish them. "It is a cruel wrong to your 'day & generation' that you will not give them light." At last Mrs. Jackson persuaded publisher Thomas Niles to include one of Emily's poems in a collection of anonymous verse, and then, prodded by Mrs. Jackson, he showed a mild interest in publishing more. But Emily's cooperation seemed only lukewarm. Perhaps Mrs. Jackson's partisanship had come too late. Perhaps the poet had taught herself to prefer a narrow audience of family and friends. And yet there is an intriguing record that for some years before her death Emily was dispatching letters and packages to yet another editor, Roswell Smith of the Century Company.

One suspects that she waxed warm and cold and warm again on the subject of publication. The theme crops up in her poems throughout her life: fame and obscurity, artistic immortality and the bird that sings to no listening ear:

> Glory is that bright tragic thing
> That for an instant
> Means Dominion –
> Warms some poor name
> That never felt the Sun,
> Gently replacing
> In oblivion –

When Emily died of Bright's disease on May 15, 1886, glory had not come. Oblivion seemed sure.

SO GIVE ME BACK TO DEATH

Emily Dickinson's funeral arrangements shocked a gossiping relative, Mrs. Eudocia Flynt: "... private, no flowers, taken to the Cemetery—by Irishmen, out of the back door, across the fields!! her request."

One of the guests was Thomas Wentworth Higginson, who recorded his impressions in his diary:

> To Amherst to the funeral of that rare & strange creature Emily Dickinson.
>
> The country exquisite, day perfect, & an atmosphere of its own, fine & strange about the whole house & grounds—a more saintly & elevated "House of Usher" ... E. D.'s face a wondrous restoration of youth ... perfect peace on the beautiful brow. ... How large a portion of the people who have interested me have passed away.

But Emily Dickinson had not passed out of Higginson's life forever. He was to be as good a friend to her in death, however reluctantly, as he had been in life, however cautiously. Four years later he was to become one of the editors of the first edition of her poems.

It was Lavinia who found them, shortly after Emily's death, in a locked box in her sister's bedroom. They had been gathered into some sixty little packets of folded sheets of paper loosely sewn together. (Other poems exist in draft form, often written thriftily on the backs of envelopes as if they had been jotted down impulsively. One can imagine them being pushed into the pocket of the white dress that still hangs in Emily's bedroom.)

Unlocking the box, lifting the lid, Lavinia discovered a collection of hundreds of poems. Beneath her hands lay her sister's life work, in unexpected profusion.

THE BEGGAR AT THE DOOR FOR FAME

What if Lavinia had simply closed the lid of the box, locked it, and stored it in the attic? What if the poetry of Emily Dickinson had never come to light?

One's shocked sense of loss is a measure of the poet's stature. Without the contents of that extraordinary box, only the work of Walt Whitman would remain in the very first rank from all the poetical outpourings of nineteenth-century America. His muscular cry would not be balanced by the clear passionate voice of the woman who saw "New Englandly."

At first glance they seem an oddly assorted pair. One thinks of Whitman as he appeared to Thoreau in 1856, sprawling in his upstairs bedroom in Brooklyn, the chamber pot under the unmade bed—and of Emily Dickinson as Higginson saw her in her father's spacious parlor in 1870: "She came to me with two day lilies, which she put in a sort of childlike way into my hand & said, 'These are my introduction.'"

And yet Emily Dickinson's pose of womanly weakness sets off the more stunningly a power that challenges Whitman's own. Her thrifty brevity and controlled intensity are no less overwhelming than his rambling expansiveness. But in her own lifetime she was to remain invisible. It was Whitman's broad-axe that swept from American parlor tables all the polite glassware of Lowell and Longfellow, Whittier and Holmes. Emerson was quick to hail Whitman as the new American voice he had been looking for, a poet who would celebrate "Our log-rolling, our stumps and their politics . . . the northern trade, the southern planting, the western clearing, Oregon and Texas." Thoreau called Whitman's *Leaves of Grass* "a great primitive poem,—an alarum or trumpet-note ringing through the American camp." But the poetry of Emily Dickinson was just as surely an expression of a developing nation. With images drawn from the provincial New England town she knew so well, from its cupboards and kitchens, gardens and orchards, mills and waterwheels, from the gear of its Yankee trades and the hooting of its railroads, she created a body of work as clear-seeing and as native as Walt Whitman's, as large and as lasting. As worthily as Whitman she might have earned Emerson's praise as a new "genius in America."

Emerson was never to know her poetry. Thoreau died in the year her flood was at its height. And when Walt Whitman wrote his *Song of the Exposition*, shouting his jubilant invitation across the Atlantic, "Come Muse migrate from Greece and Ionia," he too had no way of knowing that the muse had already migrated, that she was perched with the cherubim on the roof of a large brick house in the village of Amherst, Massachusetts.

THE BALLOTS OF ETERNITY

Lavinia, of course, did not lock the precious box of poems and put it in the attic. Astonished by the bulk of her sister's work, determined to see her memory honored by publication, she took the packets to Austin's wife next door. Susan promised to help, to go through the poems and prepare a selection for the inspection of an editor. But when Susan delayed, Vinnie took the poems back again and gave them to Mabel Loomis Todd, a sympathetic and talented young neighbor. (Mabel's love affair with Austin is another story altogether.) And it was Mabel Todd who at last persuaded a doubting Thomas Wentworth Higginson into talking an uncertain Thomas Niles of Roberts Brothers into printing a first selection of one hundred fifteen poems.

The first edition of 1890 was a success. By 1892 there had been eleven editions. By the nineteen twenties the fame of Emily Dickinson was widespread, and her reputation has grown steadily ever since.

Did Higginson ever regret his dry disparagement of the poems in Emily's lifetime? One can only fervently hope so.

> 'Tis little I – could care for Pearls –
> Who own the ample sea –

The sheer size of Emily Dickinson's production is almost baffling. Wandering among her poems is like leafing through the journals of Henry Thoreau — there is the same sense of inexhaustible luxuriance and fecundity. Some of her stanzas are queer and crabbed, many of her poems are unfinished, but among the seventeen hundred seventy-five that appear in editions of her complete works there are hundreds that can only be called masterpieces. Even her lesser poems contain enough deathless phrases to fill a small *Bartlett's Quotations*, dazzling lines that begin to stand for life experiences and illuminate undiscovered feelings.

They alone guarantee her survival. But it is not only the quotable bits and pieces that appeal to the contemporary reader. In several ways the poetry of Emily Dickinson seems ahead of its time, belonging not to her own age but to ours. Her poems of private suffering and death match a central theme of twentieth-century poetry, and her style of sharp stenographic obliqueness suits us as the magniloquence of a Lowell or Longfellow does not.

But her poetry also affects us with a special force because it expresses something that is *missing* from our own, a transfigured vision of the natural world. "The Breaking of the Day / Addeth to my Degree"; "You'll know it – as you know 'tis Noon – / By Glory": lines like these stimulate in us some shriveled organ of awareness, feeding an unconscious starvation. Her ecstatic sense of "sum" in witnessing the bird's song or the red blaze of the morning has a rare excitement for readers accustomed to a bleaker poetry of melancholy subtractions. We begin to suspect that we too have been receiving bulletins from immortality, undecipherable without her magical translation.

In the end it is perhaps their sense of vastness that carries her poems so powerfully forward into this or any other century, the immensities that spread outward from her short quatrains, the firmaments that fill her basket, her acquaintance with eternity. Veils are withdrawn from central mysteries, daily trivialities vanish in the breath of her ethereal wind, the sea parts to show a further sea. We behold the sweep of limitless space and infinite time.

POEMS

The Only News I know
Is Bulletins all Day
From Immortality.

The Only Shows I see –
Tomorrow and Today –
Perchance Eternity –

The Only One I meet
Is God – The Only Street –
Existence – This traversed

If Other News there be –
Or Admirabler Show –
I'll tell it You –

I taste a liquor never brewed–
From Tankards scooped in Pearl–
Not all the Vats upon the Rhine
Yield such an Alcohol!

Inebriate of Air–am I–
And Debauchee of Dew–
Reeling–thro endless summer days–
From inns of Molten Blue–

When "Landlords" turn the drunken Bee
Out of the Foxglove's door–
When Butterflies–renounce their "drams"–
I shall but drink the more!

Till Seraphs swing their snowy Hats–
And Saints–to windows run–
To see the little Tippler
Leaning against the–Sun–

This is my letter to the World
That never wrote to Me –
The simple News that Nature told –
With tender Majesty

Her message is committed
To Hands I cannot see –
For love of Her – Sweet – countrymen –
Judge tenderly – of Me

The Mountain sat upon the Plain
In his tremendous Chair –
His observation omnifold,
His inquest, everywhere –

The Seasons played around his knees
Like Children round a sire –
Grandfather of the Days is He
Of Dawn, the Ancestor –

Sweet is the swamp with its secrets,
Until we meet a snake;
'Tis then we sigh for houses,
And our departure take

At that enthralling gallop
That only childhood knows.
A snake is summer's treason,
And guile is where it goes.

Carlo Dreams

Of all the Sounds despatched abroad,
There's not a Charge to me
Like that old measure in the Boughs–
That phraseless Melody–
The Wind does–working like a Hand,
Whose fingers Comb the Sky–
Then quiver down–with tufts of Tune–
Permitted Gods, and me–

Inheritance, it is, to us–
Beyond the Art to Earn–
Beyond the trait to take away
By Robber, since the Gain
Is gotten not of fingers–
And inner than the Bone–
Hid golden, for the whole of Days,
And even in the Urn,
I cannot vouch the merry Dust
Do not arise and play
In some odd fashion of its own,
Some quainter Holiday,
When Winds go round and round in Bands–
And thrum upon the door,
And Birds take places, overhead,
To bear them Orchestra.

I crave Him grace of Summer Boughs,
If such an Outcast be–
Who never heard that fleshless Chant–
Rise–solemn–on the Tree,
As if some Caravan of Sound
Off Deserts, in the Sky,
Had parted Rank,
Then knit, and swept–
In Seamless Company–

The Robin's my Criterion for Tune–
Because I grow–where Robins do–
But, were I Cuckoo born–
I'd swear by him–
The ode familiar–rules the Noon–
The Buttercup's, my Whim for Bloom–
Because, we're Orchard sprung–
But, were I Britain born,
I'd Daisies spurn–
None but the Nut–October fit–
Because, through dropping it,
The Seasons flit–I'm taught–
Without the Snow's Tableau
Winter, were lie–to me–
Because I see–New Englandly–
The Queen, discerns like me–
Provincially–

Exultation is the going
Of an inland soul to sea,
Past the houses–past the headlands–
Into deep Eternity–

Bred as we, among the mountains,
Can the sailor understand
The divine intoxication
Of the first league out from land?

A something in a summer's Day
As slow her flambeaux burn away
Which solemnizes me.

A something in a summer's noon—
A depth—an Azure—a perfume—
Transcending ecstasy.

And still within a summer's night
A something so transporting bright
I clap my hands to see—

Then veil my too inspecting face
Lest such a subtle—shimmering grace
Flutter too far for me—

The wizard fingers never rest—
The purple brook within the breast
Still chafes its narrow bed—

Still rears the East her amber Flag—
Guides still the Sun along the Crag
His Caravan of Red—

So looking on—the night—the morn
Conclude the wonder gay—
And I meet, coming thro' the dews
Another summer's Day!

Beauty–be not caused–It Is–
Chase it, and it ceases–
Chase it not, and it abides–

Overtake the Creases

In the Meadow–when the Wind
Runs his fingers thro' it–
Deity will see to it
That You never do it–

The Red—Blaze—is the Morning—
The Violet—is Noon—
The Yellow—Day—is falling—
And after that—is none—

But Miles of Sparks—at Evening—
Reveal the Width that burned—
The Territory Argent—that
Never yet—consumed—

Noon—is the Hinge of Day—
Evening—the Tissue Door—
Morning—the East compelling the sill
Till all the World is ajar—

The Soul's distinct connection
With immortality
Is best disclosed by Danger
Or quick Calamity –

As Lightning on a Landscape
Exhibits Sheets of Place –
Not yet suspected – but for Flash –
And Click – and Suddenness.

Two Butterflies went out at Noon–
And waltzed upon a Farm–
Then stepped straight through the Firmament
And rested, on a Beam–

And then–together bore away
Upon a shining Sea–
Though never yet, in any Port–
Their coming, mentioned–be–

If spoken by the distant Bird–
If met in Ether Sea
By Frigate, or by Merchantman–
No notice–was–to me–

Four Trees–upon a solitary Acre–
Without Design
Or Order, or Apparent Action–
Maintain–

The Sun–upon a Morning meets them–
The Wind–
No nearer Neighbor–have they–
But God–

The Acre gives them–Place–
They–Him–Attention of Passer by–
Of Shadow, or of Squirrel, haply–
Or Boy–

What Deed is Theirs unto the General Nature–
What Plan
They severally–retard–or further–
Unknown–

The Lilac is an ancient shrub
But ancienter than that
The Firmamental Lilac
Upon the Hill tonight–
The Sun subsiding on his Course
Bequeaths this final Plant
To Contemplation–not to Touch–
The Flower of Occident.
Of one Corolla is the West–
The Calyx is the Earth–
The Capsules burnished Seeds the Stars
The Scientist of Faith
His research has but just begun–
Above his synthesis
The Flora unimpeachable
To Time's Analysis–
"Eye hath not seen" may possibly
Be current with the Blind
But let not Revelation
By theses be detained–

Perhaps I asked too large–
I take–no less than skies–
For Earths, grow thick as
Berries, in my native town–

My Basket holds–just–Firmaments–
Those–dangle easy–on my arm,
But smaller bundles–Cram.

"*East*"

Tell all the Truth but tell it slant–
Success in Circuit lies
Too bright for our infirm Delight
The Truth's superb surprise

As Lightning to the Children eased
With explanation kind
The Truth must dazzle gradually
Or every man be blind–

The Outer–from the Inner
Derives its Magnitude–
'Tis Duke, or Dwarf, according
As is the Central Mood–

The fine–unvarying Axis
That regulates the Wheel–
Though Spokes–spin–more conspicuous
And fling a dust–the while.

The Inner–paints the Outer–
The Brush without the Hand–
Its Picture publishes–precise–
As is the inner Brand–

On fine–Arterial Canvas–
A Cheek–perchance a Brow–
The Star's whole Secret–in the Lake–
Eyes were not meant to know.

The Way I read a Letter's–this–
'Tis first–I lock the Door–
And push it with my fingers–next–
For transport it be sure–

And then I go the furthest off
To counteract a knock–
Then draw my little Letter forth
And slowly pick the lock–

Then–glancing narrow, at the Wall–
And narrow at the floor
For firm Conviction of a Mouse
Not exorcised before–

Peruse how infinite I am
To no one that You–know–
And sigh for lack of Heaven–but not
The Heaven God bestow–

I envy Seas, whereon He rides–
I envy Spokes of Wheels
Of Chariots, that Him convey–
I envy Crooked Hills

That gaze upon His journey–
How easy All can see
What is forbidden utterly
As Heaven–unto me!

I envy Nests of Sparrows–
That dot His distant Eaves–
The wealthy Fly, upon His Pane–
The happy–happy Leaves–

That just abroad His Window
Have Summer's leave to play–
The Ear Rings of Pizarro
Could not obtain for me–

I envy Light–that wakes Him–
And Bells–that boldly ring
To tell Him it is Noon, abroad–
Myself–be Noon to Him–

Yet interdict–my Blossom–
And abrogate–my Bee–
Lest Noon in Everlasting Night–
Drop Gabriel–and Me–

Of all the Souls that stand create—
I have elected—One—
When Sense from Spirit—files away—
And Subterfuge—is done—
When that which is—and that which was—
Apart—intrinsic—stand—
And this brief Drama in the flesh—
Is shifted—like a Sand—
When Figures show their royal Front—
And Mists—are carved away,
Behold the Atom—I preferred—
To all the lists of Clay!

"Why do I love" You, Sir?
Because –
The Wind does not require the Grass
To answer – Wherefore when He pass
She cannot keep Her place.

Because He knows – and
Do not You –
And We know not –
Enough for Us
The Wisdom it be so –

The Lightning – never asked an Eye
Wherefore it shut – when He was by –
Because He knows it cannot speak –
And reasons not contained –
– Of Talk –
There be – preferred by Daintier Folk –

The Sunrise – Sir – compelleth Me –
Because He's Sunrise – and I see –
Therefore – Then –
I love Thee –

I started Early–Took my Dog–
And visited the Sea–
The Mermaids in the Basement
Came out to look at me–

And Frigates–in the Upper Floor
Extended Hempen Hands–
Presuming Me to be a Mouse–
Aground–upon the Sands–

But no Man moved Me–till the Tide
Went past my simple Shoe–
And past my Apron–and my Belt
And past my Bodice–too–

And made as He would eat me up–
As wholly as a Dew
Upon a Dandelion's Sleeve–
And then–I started–too–

And He–He followed–close behind–
I felt His Silver Heel
Upon my Ankle–Then my Shoes
Would overflow with Pearl–

Until We met the Solid Town–
No One He seemed to know–
And bowing–with a Mighty look–
At me–The Sea withdrew–

We miss a Kinsman more
When warranted to see
Than when withheld of Oceans
From possibility

A Furlong than a League
Inflicts a pricklier pain,
Till We, who smiled at Pyrenees—
Of Parishes, complain.

If you were coming in the Fall,
I'd brush the Summer by
With half a smile, and half a spurn,
As Housewives do, a Fly.

If I could see you in a year,
I'd wind the months in balls–
And put them each in separate Drawers,
For fear the numbers fuse–

If only Centuries, delayed,
I'd count them on my Hand,
Subtracting, till my fingers dropped
Into Van Dieman's Land.

If certain, when this life was out–
That yours and mine, should be–
I'd toss it yonder, like a Rind,
And take Eternity–

But, now, uncertain of the length
Of this, that is between,
It goads me, like the Goblin Bee–
That will not state–its sting.

There came a Day at Summer's full,
Entirely for me—
I thought that such were for the Saints,
Where Resurrections—be—

The Sun, as common, went abroad,
The flowers, accustomed, blew,
As if no soul the solstice passed
That maketh all things new—

The time was scarce profaned, by speech—
The symbol of a word
Was needless, as at Sacrament,
The Wardrobe—of our Lord—

Each was to each The Sealed Church,
Permitted to commune this—time—
Lest we too awkward show
At Supper of the Lamb.

The Hours slid fast–as Hours will,
Clutched tight, by greedy hands–
So faces on two Decks, look back,
Bound to opposing lands–

And so when all the time had leaked,
Without external sound
Each bound the Other's Crucifix–
We gave no other Bond–

Sufficient troth, that we shall rise–
Deposed–at length, the Grave–
To that new Marriage,
Justified–through Calvaries of Love–

Earthlight

Mine–by the Right of the White Election!
Mine–by the Royal Seal!
Mine–by the Sign in the Scarlet prison–
Bars–cannot conceal!

Mine–here–in Vision –and in Veto!
Mine–by the Grave's Repeal–
Titled–Confirmed–
Delirious Charter!
Mine–long as Ages steal!

Again–his voice is at the door–
I feel the old *Degree*–
I hear him ask the servant
For such an one–as me–

I take a *flower*–as I go–
My face to *justify*–
He never *saw* me–*in this life*–
I might *surprise* his eye!

I cross the Hall with *mingled* steps–
I–silent–pass the door–
I look on all this world *contains*–
Just his face–nothing more!

We talk in *careless*–and in *toss*–
A kind of *plummet* strain–
Each–sounding–shyly–
Just–how–deep–
The *other's* one–had been–

We *walk*–I leave my Dog–at home–
A *tender*–*thoughtful* Moon
Goes with us–just a little way–
And–then–we are *alone*–

Alone–if *Angels* are "alone"–
First time they *try* the *sky*!
Alone–if those "veiled faces"–be–
We cannot *count*–on High!

I'd give–to live that hour–*again*–
The *purple*–*in my Vein*–
But *He* must *count the drops*–*himself*–
My price for *every stain*!

The Zeroes–taught us–Phosphorus–
We learned to like the Fire
By playing Glaciers–when a Boy–
And Tinder–guessed–by power
Of Opposite–to balance Odd–
If White–a Red–must be!
Paralysis–our Primer–dumb–
Unto Vitality!

Presentiment–is that long Shadow–on the Lawn–
Indicative that Suns go down–

The Notice to the startled Grass
That Darkness–is about to pass–

I cannot live with You–
It would be Life–
And Life is over there–
Behind the Shelf

The Sexton keeps the Key to–
Putting up
Our Life–His Porcelain–
Like a Cup–

Discarded of the Housewife–
Quaint–or Broke–
A newer Sevres pleases–
Old Ones crack–

I could not die–with You–
For One must wait
To shut the Other's Gaze down–
You–could not–

And I–Could I stand by
And see You–freeze–
Without my Right of Frost–
Death's privilege?

Nor could I rise–with You–
Because Your Face
Would put out Jesus'–
That New Grace

Glow plain—and foreign
On my homesick Eye—
Except that You than He
Shone closer by—

They'd judge Us—How—
For You—served Heaven—You know,
Or sought to—
I could not—

Because You saturated Sight—
And I had no more Eyes
For sordid excellence
As Paradise

And were You lost, I would be—
Though My Name
Rang loudest
On the Heavenly fame—

And were You—saved—
And I—condemned to be
Where You were not—
That self—were Hell to Me—

So We must meet apart—
You there—I—here—
With just the Door ajar
That Oceans are—and Prayer—
And that White Sustenance—
Despair—

A great Hope fell
You heard no noise
The Ruin was within
Oh cunning wreck that told no tale
And let no Witness in

The mind was built for mighty Freight
For dread occasion planned
How often foundering at Sea
Ostensibly, on Land

A not admitting of the wound
Until it grew so wide
That all my Life had entered it
And there were troughs beside

A closing of the simple lid
That opened to the sun
Until the tender Carpenter
Perpetual nail it down–

I felt a Funeral, in my Brain,
And Mourners to and fro
Kept treading–treading–till it seemed
That Sense was breaking through–

And when they all were seated,
A Service, like a Drum–
Kept beating–beating–till I thought
My Mind was going numb–

And then I heard them lift a Box
And creak across my Soul
With those same Boots of Lead, again,
Then Space–began to toll,

As all the Heavens were a Bell,
And Being, but an Ear,
And I, and Silence, some strange Race
Wrecked, solitary, here–

And then a Plank in Reason, broke,
And I dropped down, and down–
And hit a World, at every plunge,
And Finished knowing–then–

I heard a Fly buzz–when I died–
The Stillness in the Room
Was like the Stillness in the Air–
Between the Heaves of Storm–

The Eyes around–had wrung them dry–
And Breaths were gathering firm
For that last Onset–when the King
Be witnessed–in the Room–

I willed my Keepsakes–Signed away
What portion of me be
Assignable–and then it was
There interposed a Fly–

With Blue–uncertain stumbling Buzz–
Between the light–and me–
And then the Windows failed–and then
I could not see to see–

Ample make this Bed–
Make this Bed with Awe–
In it wait till Judgment break
Excellent and Fair.

Be its Mattress straight–
Be its Pillow round–
Let no Sunrise' yellow noise
Interrupt this Ground–

A Landscape So Lone

Just lost, when I was saved!
Just felt the world go by!
Just girt me for the onset with Eternity,
When breath blew back,
And on the other side
I heard recede the disappointed tide!

Therefore, as One returned, I feel
Odd secrets of the line to tell!
Some Sailor, skirting foreign shores–
Some pale Reporter, from the awful doors
Before the Seal!

Next time, to stay!
Next time, the things to see
By Ear unheard,
Unscrutinized by Eye–

Next time, to tarry,
While the Ages steal–
Slow tramp the Centuries,
And the Cycles wheel!

Crumbling is not an instant's Act
A fundamental pause
Dilapidation's processes
Are organized Decays.

'Tis first a Cobweb on the Soul
A Cuticle of Dust
A Borer in the Axis
An Elemental Rust–

Ruin is formal–Devil's work
Consecutive and slow–
Fail in an instant, no man did
Slipping–is Crash's law.

I've known a Heaven, like a Tent—
To wrap its shining Yards—
Pluck up its stakes, and disappear—
Without the sound of Boards
Or Rip of Nail—Or Carpenter—
But just the miles of stare—
That signalize a Show's Retreat—
In North America—

No Trace—no Figment of the Thing
That dazzled, Yesterday,
No Ring—no Marvel—
Men, and Feats—
Dissolved as utterly—
As Bird's far Navigation
Discloses just a Hue—
A plash of Oars, a Gaiety—
Then swallowed up, of View.

The Soul selects her own Society—
Then—shuts the Door—
To her divine Majority—
Present no more—

Unmoved—she notes the Chariots—pausing—
At her low Gate—
Unmoved—an Emperor be kneeling
Upon her Mat—

I've known her—from an ample nation—
Choose One—
Then—close the Valves of her attention—
Like Stone—

Prayer is the little implement
Through which Men reach
Where Presence–is denied them.
They fling their Speech

By means of it–in God's Ear–
If then He hear–
This sums the Apparatus
Comprised in Prayer–

It's easy to invent a Life–
God does it–every Day–
Creation–but the Gambol
Of His Authority–

It's easy to efface it–
The thrifty Deity
Could scarce afford Eternity
To Spontaneity–

The Perished Patterns murmur–
But His Perturbless Plan
Proceed–inserting Here–a Sun–
There–leaving out a Man–

After great pain, a formal feeling comes–
The Nerves sit ceremonious, like Tombs–
The stiff Heart questions was it He, that bore,
And Yesterday, or Centuries before?

The Feet, mechanical, go round–
A Wooden way
Of Ground, or Air, or Ought–
Regardless grown,
A Quartz contentment, like a stone–

This is the Hour of Lead–
Remembered, if outlived,
As Freezing persons, recollect the Snow–
First–Chill–then Stupor–then the letting go–

I got so I could take his name–
Without–Tremendous gain–
That Stop-sensation–on my Soul–
And Thunder–in the Room–

I got so I could walk across
That Angle in the floor,
Where he turned so, and I turned–how–
And all our Sinew tore–

I got so I could stir the Box–
In which his letters grew
Without that forcing, in my breath–
As Staples–driven through–

Could dimly recollect a Grace–
I think, they call it "God"–
Renowned to ease Extremity–
When Formula, had failed–

And shape my Hands–
Petition's way,
Tho' ignorant of a word
That Ordination–utters–

My Business, with the Cloud,
If any Power behind it, be,
Not subject to Despair–
It care, in some remoter way,
For so minute affair
As Misery–
Itself, too vast, for interrupting–more–

There's a certain Slant of light,
Winter Afternoons–
That oppresses, like the Heft
Of Cathedral Tunes–

Heavenly Hurt, it gives us–
We can find no scar,
But internal difference,
Where the Meanings, are–

None may teach it–Any–
'Tis the Seal Despair–
An imperial affliction
Sent us of the Air–

When it comes, the Landscape listens–
Shadows–hold their breath–
When it goes, 'tis like the Distance
On the look of Death–

Dare you see a Soul *at the White Heat?*
Then crouch within the door–
Red–is the Fire's common tint–
But when the vivid Ore
Has vanquished Flame's conditions,
It quivers from the Forge
Without a color, but the light
Of unanointed Blaze.
Least Village has its Blacksmith
Whose Anvil's even ring
Stands symbol for the finer Forge
That soundless tugs–within–
Refining these impatient Ores
With Hammer, and with Blaze
Until the Designated Light
Repudiate the Forge–

I stepped from Plank to Plank
A slow and cautious way
The Stars about my Head I felt
About my Feet the Sea.

I knew not but the next
Would be my final inch–
This gave me that precarious Gait
Some call Experience.

There came a Wind like a Bugle–
It quivered through the Grass
And a Green Chill upon the Heat
So ominous did pass
We barred the Windows and the Doors
As from an Emerald Ghost–
The Doom's electric Moccasin
That very instant passed–
On a strange Mob of panting Trees
And Fences fled away
And Rivers where the Houses ran
Those looked that lived–that Day–
The Bell within the steeple wild
The flying tidings told–
How much can come
And much can go,
And yet abide the World!

Of Stir and Place

Down Time's quaint stream
Without an oar
We are enforced to sail
Our Port a secret
Our Perchance a Gale
What Skipper would
Incur the Risk
What Buccaneer would ride
Without a surety from the Wind
Or schedule of the Tide—

White as an Indian Pipe
Red as a Cardinal Flower
Fabulous as a Moon at Noon
February Hour–

A prompt–executive Bird is the Jay–
Bold as a Bailiff's Hymn–
Brittle and Brief in quality–
Warrant in every line–

Sitting a Bough like a Brigadier
Confident and straight–
Much is the mien of him in March
As a Magistrate–

By my Window have I for Scenery
Just a Sea—with a Stem—
If the Bird and the Farmer—deem it a "Pine"—
The Opinion will serve—for them—

It has no Port, nor a "Line"—but the Jays—
That split their route to the Sky—
Or a Squirrel, whose giddy Peninsula
May be easier reached—this way—

For Inlands—the Earth is the under side—
And the upper side—is the Sun—
And its Commerce—if Commerce it have—
Of Spice—I infer from the Odors borne—

Of its Voice–to affirm–when the Wind is within–
Can the Dumb–define the Divine?
The Definition of Melody–is–
That Definition is none–

It–suggests to our Faith–
They–suggest to our Sight–
When the latter–is put away
I shall meet with Conviction I somewhere met
That Immortality–

Was the Pine at my Window a "Fellow
Of the Royal" Infinity?
Apprehensions–are God's introductions–
To be hallowed–accordingly–

Beauty crowds me till I die
Beauty mercy have on me
But if I expire today
Let it be in sight of thee–

The Dandelion's pallid tube
Astonishes the Grass,
And Winter instantly becomes
An infinite Alas–

The tube uplifts a signal Bud
And then a shouting Flower,–
The Proclamation of the Suns
That sepulture is o'er.

Bee! I'm expecting you!
Was saying Yesterday
To Somebody you know
That you were due–

The Frogs got Home last Week–
Are settled, and at work–
Birds, mostly back–
The Clover warm and thick–

You'll get my Letter by
The seventeenth; Reply
Or better, be with me–
Yours, Fly.

Pink—small—and punctual—
Aromatic—low—
Covert—in April—
Candid—in May—
Dear to the Moss—
Known to the Knoll—
Next to the Robin
In every human Soul—
Bold little Beauty
Bedecked with thee
Nature forswears
Antiquity—

The Bat is dun, with wrinkled Wings—
Like fallow Article—
And not a song pervade his Lips—
Or none perceptible.

His small Umbrella quaintly halved
Describing in the Air
An Arc alike inscrutable
Elate Philosopher.

Deputed from what Firmament—
Of what Astute Abode—
Empowered with what Malignity
Auspiciously withheld—

To his adroit Creator
Ascribe no less the praise—
Beneficent, believe me,
His Eccentricities—

These are the Nights that Beetles love—
From Eminence remote
Drives ponderous perpendicular
His figure intimate
The terror of the Children
The merriment of men
Depositing his Thunder
He hoists abroad again—
A Bomb upon the Ceiling
Is an improving thing—
It keeps the nerves progressive
Conjecture flourishing—
Too dear the Summer evening
Without discreet alarm—
Supplied by Entomology
With its remaining charm—

"Much Bouquet"

Between My Country—and the Others—
There is a Sea—
But Flowers—negotiate between us—
As Ministry.

The Crickets sang
And set the Sun
And Workmen finished one by one
Their Seam the Day upon.

The low Grass loaded with the Dew
The Twilight stood, as Strangers do
With Hat in Hand, polite and new
To stay as if, or go.

A Vastness, as a Neighbor, came,
A Wisdom, without Face, or Name,
A Peace, as Hemispheres at Home
And so the Night became.

One of the ones that Midas touched
Who failed to touch us all
Was that confiding Prodigal
The reeling Oriole–

So drunk he disavows it
With badinage divine–
So dazzling we mistake him
For an alighting Mine–

A Pleader–a Dissembler–
An Epicure–a Thief–
Betimes an Oratorio–
An Ecstasy in chief–

The Jesuit of Orchards
He cheats as he enchants
Of an entire Attar
For his decamping wants–

The splendor of a Burmah
The Meteor of Birds,
Departing like a Pageant
Of Ballads and of Bards–

I never thought that Jason sought
For any Golden Fleece
But then I am a rural man
With thoughts that make for Peace–

But if there were a Jason,
Tradition bear with me
Behold his lost Aggrandizement
Upon the Apple Tree–

Bees are Black, with Gilt Surcingles—
Buccaneers of Buzz.
Ride abroad in ostentation
And subsist on Fuzz.

Fuzz ordained—not Fuzz contingent—
Marrows of the Hill.
Jugs—a Universe's fracture
Could not jar or spill.

Before the ice is in the pools—
Before the skaters go,
Or any cheek at nightfall
Is tarnished by the snow—

Before the fields have finished,
Before the Christmas tree,
Wonder upon wonder
Will arrive to me!

What we touch the hems of
On a summer's day—
What is only walking
Just a bridge away—

That which sings so—speaks so—
When there's no one here—
Will the frock I wept in
Answer me to wear?

These are the days when Birds come back—
A very few—a Bird or two—
To take a backward look.

These are the days when skies resume
The old—old sophistries of June—
A blue and gold mistake.

Oh fraud that cannot cheat the Bee—
Almost thy plausibility
Induces my belief.

Till ranks of seeds their witness bear—
And softly thro' the altered air
Hurries a timid leaf.

Oh Sacrament of summer days,
Oh Last Communion in the Haze—
Permit a child to join.

Thy sacred emblems to partake—
Thy consecrated bread to take
And thine immortal wine!

Essential Oils—are wrung—
The Attar from the Rose
Be not expressed by Suns—alone—
It is the gift of Screws—

The General Rose—decay—
But this—in Lady's Drawer
Make Summer—When the Lady lie
In Ceaseless Rosemary—

I reckon–when I count at all–
First–Poets–Then the Sun –
Then Summer–Then the Heaven of God–
And then–the List is done–

But, looking back–the First so seems
To Comprehend the Whole–
The Others look a needless Show–
So I write–Poets–All–

Their Summer–lasts a Solid Year–
They can afford a Sun
The East–would deem extravagant–
And if the Further Heaven–

Be Beautiful as they prepare
For Those who worship Them–
It is too difficult a Grace–
To justify the Dream–

I send Two Sunsets–
Day and I–in competition ran–
I finished Two–and several Stars–
While He–was making One–

His own was ampler–but as I
Was saying to a friend–
Mine–is the more convenient
To Carry in the Hand–

The Truth–is stirless–
Other force–may be presumed to move–
This–then–is best for confidence–
When oldest Cedars swerve–

And Oaks untwist their fists–
And Mountains–feeble–lean–
How excellent a Body, that
Stands without a Bone–

How vigorous a Force
That holds without a Prop–
Truth stays Herself–and every man
That trusts Her–boldly up–

The Brain–is wider than the Sky–
For–put them side by side–
The one the other will contain
With ease–and You–beside–

The Brain is deeper than the sea–
For–hold them–Blue to Blue–
The one the other will absorb–
As Sponges–Buckets–do–

The Brain is just the weight of God–
For–Heft them–Pound for Pound–
And they will differ–if they do–
As Syllable from Sound–

"Image of Light"

The farthest Thunder that I heard
Was nearer than the Sky
And rumbles still, though torrid Noons
Have lain their missiles by—
The Lightning that preceded it
Struck no one but myself—
But I would not exchange the Bolt
For all the rest of Life—
Indebtedness to Oxygen
The Happy may repay,
But not the obligation
To Electricity—
It founds the Homes and decks the Days
And every clamor bright
Is but the gleam concomitant
Of that waylaying Light—
The Thought is quiet as a Flake—
A Crash without a Sound,
How Life's reverberation
Its Explanation found—

The Poets light but Lamps–
Themselves–go out–
The Wicks they stimulate–
If vital Light

Inhere as do the Suns–
Each Age a Lens
Disseminating their
Circumference–

On a Columnar Self–
How ample to rely
In Tumult–or Extremity–
How good the Certainty

That Lever cannot pry–
And Wedge cannot divide
Conviction–That Granitic Base–
Though None be on our Side–

Suffice Us–for a Crowd–
Ourself–and Rectitude–
And that Assembly–not far off
From furthest Spirit–God–

There is no Frigate like a Book
To take us Lands away
Nor any Coursers like a Page
Of prancing Poetry—
This Traverse may the poorest take
Without oppress of Toll—
How frugal is the Chariot
That bears the Human soul.

Long Years apart—can make no
Breach a second cannot fill—
The absence of the Witch does not
Invalidate the spell—

The embers of a Thousand Years
Uncovered by the Hand
That fondled them when they were Fire
Will stir and understand—

The feet of people walking home
With gayer sandals go—
The Crocus—till she rises
The Vassal of the snow—
The lips at Hallelujah
Long years of practise bore
Till bye and bye these Bargemen
Walked singing on the shore.

Pearls are the Diver's farthings
Extorted from the Sea—
Pinions—the Seraph's wagon
Pedestrian once—as we—
Night is the morning's Canvas
Larceny—legacy—
Death, but our rapt attention
To Immortality.

My figures fail to tell me
How far the Village lies—
Whose peasants are the Angels—
Whose Cantons dot the skies—
My Classics veil their faces—
My faith that Dark adores—
Which from its solemn abbeys
Such resurrection pours.

Under the Light, yet under,
Under the Grass and the Dirt,
Under the Beetle's Cellar
Under the Clover's Root,

Further than Arm could stretch
Were it Giant long,
Further than Sunshine could
Were the Day Year long,

Over the Light, yet over,
Over the Arc of the Bird—
Over the Comet's chimney—
Over the Cubit's Head,

Further than Guess can gallop
Further than Riddle ride—
Oh for a Disc to the Distance
Between Ourselves and the Dead!

"Sweet Velocity"

Because I could not stop for Death—
He kindly stopped for me—
The Carriage held but just Ourselves—
And Immortality.

We slowly drove—He knew no haste
And I had put away
My labor and my leisure too,
For His Civility—

We passed the School, where Children strove
At Recess—in the Ring—
We passed the Fields of Gazing Grain—
We passed the Setting Sun—

Or rather—He passed Us—
The Dews drew quivering and chill—
For only Gossamer, my Gown—
My Tippet—only Tulle—

We paused before a House that seemed
A Swelling of the Ground—
The Roof was scarcely visible—
The Cornice—in the Ground—

Since then—'tis Centuries—and yet
Feels shorter than the Day
I first surmised the Horses' Heads
Were toward Eternity—

As if the Sea should part
And show a further Sea–
And that–a further–and the Three
But a presumption be–

Of Periods of Seas–
Unvisited of Shores–
Themselves the Verge of Seas to be–
Eternity–is Those–

At Half past Three, a single Bird
Unto a silent Sky
Propounded but a single term
Of cautious melody.

At Half past Four, Experiment
Had subjugated test
And lo, Her silver Principle
Supplanted all the rest.

At Half past Seven, Element
Nor Implement, be seen –
And Place was where the Presence was
Circumference between.

Progression

NOTES AND SOURCES

NOTES

ACTS OF LIGHT: "Thank you for all the Acts of Light which beautified a Summer now past to it's reward." Johnson letter 951 (from Emily Dickinson to Mrs. John Howard Sweetser, 1884)

PAGE 1   Just after we passed Mr Clapps: Leyda I: 20 (letter of Lavinia Norcross)
Oh a very great town is this!: letter 29 (to Joel Norcross, 1850)

2   there is something a going on: Leyda I: 320 (letter of Mrs. Elizabeth Hannum)
The only news I know: poem 827, lines 1–6
Daughters should be well instructed: Leyda I: 17–18
We have a very fine school: letter 6 (to Abiah Root, 1845)
At 6. oclock we all rise: letter 18 (to Abiah Root, 1847)

3   *Candy Pulling!!*: Leyda I: 167
general uproar: letter 30 (to Jane Humphrey, 1850)
Amherst is alive with fun: letter 29 (to Joel Norcross, 1850)
While I washed the dishes: letter 36 (to Abiah Root, 1850)
I am confided in by one: Leyda I: 183
Our house is crowded daily: letter 128 (to Austin Dickinson, 1853)

4   grand Republican rally: Leyda II: 133

5   Father was as usual, Chief Marshal: letter 127 (to Austin Dickinson, 1853)
nothing human shall stop me: Leyda I: 30
I like the battle of business: Sewall I: 47
it Cost him I understood: Leyda I: 339 (letter of Mrs. Elizabeth Hannum)
His heart . . . was "vast": poem 1312
pure and terrible: letter 418 (to T. W. Higginson, 1874)
Father steps like Cromwell: letter 339 (to Louise and Frances Norcross, 1870)
Oh! dear!: Sewall I: 63

6   if we had come up . . . from two wells: Sewall I: 151 (letter to Joseph Lyman)
Emily "had to think": Sewall I: 128
I feel the oddest fright: letter 200 (to Mrs. Joseph Haven, 1859)
How do most people live: Leyda II: 151 (quoted by T. W. Higginson, 1870)

7   the noiseless noise: letter 271 (to T. W. Higginson, 1862)
very showy black horse: Leyda II: 126

7   one large part of the business: Leyda I: 88
    Friday I tasted life: letter 318 (to Mrs. J. G. Holland, 1866)
    meeting a God face to face: Leyda I: 351

8   they joggle the mind: letter 261 (to T. W. Higginson, 1862)
    Strong draughts of their refreshing minds: poem 711, lines 1–5
    Menagerie to me: poem 1206, lines 3–4
    I know of no choicer ecstasy: letter 389 (to Louise and Frances Norcross, 1873)
    I am already set down: letter 30 (to Jane Humphrey, 1850)

9   devoured the luscious passages; I thought: Sewall II: 669
    I do not cross my Father's ground: letter 330 (to T. W. Higginson, 1869)
    Soil of flint: poem 681, lines 1–2

10 They are religious—except me: letter 261 (to T. W. Higginson, 1862)
    priest factory: Sewall I: 34
    the faces of good men shine: letter 35 (to Jane Humphrey, 1850)
    His pastor said to him: Sewall I: 66
    Oh! Austin . . . How beautiful: Leyda I: 170
    They hunted high and low: Leyda II: 478
    Our sick one still lingers: Leyda I: 145

11 Miss Lyon . . . asked all those: Leyda I: 136
    I regret that last term: letter 23 (to Abiah Root, 1848)
    The earth and I, alone: poem 1079, line 2
    Give me the obscure life: Henry D. Thoreau, *Journal*: August 28, 1851
    Not "Revelation"–'tis–that waits: poem 685

12 I think I was enchanted: poem 593, lines 1–8, 17–32

13 I taste a liquor: poem 214, lines 1–8
    To have such sweet impressions: Thoreau, *Journal*: July 16, 1851

14 self-appointed inspector: Henry D. Thoreau, *Walden* (Princeton, New Jersey: Princeton
        University Press, 1971), p. 18
    It is true, I never assisted: ibid., p. 17
    Nature . . . plays without a friend: letter 319 (to T. W. Higginson, 1866)
    The sun went down: poem 1079, lines 1–3
    We like March: poem 1213 (version of 1878)

15 Nature is a Haunted House: Sewall II: 567n
    I do not respect "doctrines": letter 200 (to Mrs. Joseph Haven, 1859)
    You'll know it–as you know 'tis noon: poem 420
    The fact that earth is heaven: poem 1408, lines 1–2

16 As if the sea should part: poem 695
    No friend have I: poem 1684, lines 7–8
    Her basket, she said, held firmaments: cf. poem 352
    Gamuts of eternities: poem 967, line 7
    Meadows of majesty; easy sweeps of sky: poem 1099, lines 7, 8
    Upon his saddle sprung a bird: poem 1600

17 Beauty crowds me: poem 1654
    On twigs of singing: poem 373, line 17
    Why should I feel lonely: Thoreau, *Walden*, p. 133
    The name of it is love: poem 1438, line 4
    There, marriage is like that: Thoreau, in Walter Harding, *The Days of Henry Thoreau* (New
        York: Alfred A. Knopf, 1965), p. 110

And now another friendship is ended: Thoreau, *Journal*: February 8, 1857

18 Master . . . if I wish with a might: letter 233 (about 1861)
the wealthy fly: poem 498, line 11
Forever at his side: poem 246, lines 1–5

19 Title divine – is mine: poem 1072, lines 1–4, 13–15 (in letter 250 to Samuel Bowles, early 1862)
If you doubted my snow: letter 251 (to Samuel Bowles, early 1862)
mute inglorious Miltons: Sewall II: 539
wonderful effusions: Leyda II: 55
Are you too deeply occupied: letter 260 (to T. W. Higginson, 1862)
strange power: Leyda II: 137

20 Preceptor; in the dark: letter 265 (to T. W. Higginson, 1862)
You left me – sire – two legacies: poem 644
blister: poem 296
stabbed: poem 497
scalds: poem 193
gimlets – among the nerve: poem 244, line 6
I tie my hat: poem 443, lines 1–12

21 Limit – how deep: poem 269, lines 3–6
Sharp pittances of years: poem 125, lines 6–8
Come slowly – Eden: poem 211

22 Dont you know you are happiest: letter 562 (to Otis P. Lord, about 1878)

23 malarial Typhoid: Leyda II: 407
I see him in the star: letter 868 (to Susan Dickinson, 1883)
is there more?: letter 873 (to Mrs. J. G. Holland, 1883)
Death, whose if is everlasting: Leyda II: 424
They dropped like flakes: poem 409, lines 1–5
A single screw of flesh: poem 263, lines 1–2
Death is not destruction: Leyda II: 262 (sermon of Charles Wadsworth, 1876)
still the tooth: poem 501, lines 19–20
Bareheaded life: letter 220 (to Samuel Bowles, about 1860)
You mention Immortality: letter 319 (to T. W. Higginson, 1866)

24 Once to achieve: poem 922, lines 7–8
Abyss has no biographer: letter 899 (to Martha Gilbert Smith, about 1884)
Affidavit: poem 1408
kindly stopped for me: poem 712, line 2
that drowsy route: poem 1662, lines 1–2
lean against the Grave: poem 292, line 3
the supple suitor: poem 1445, line 1
hospitable pall: poem 1626, line 6
cordial grave: poem 1625, line 1
Obsequious angels, royal retinue: poem 171, lines 10, 11
A pit – but Heaven over it: poem 1712, lines 1–6
Escape – it is the basket: poem 1347, lines 5–8

25 shall not tell: poem 1326, lines 2, 3
the if of deity; Death, whose if: Leyda II: 424
My business is circumference: letter 268 (to T. W. Higginson, 1862)
She staked her feathers: poem 798
hasps of steel: poem 187, line 4

26   It was given to me by the Gods; I kept it in my hand: poem 454, lines 1–2, 5–8
reduceless mine, estate perpetual: poem 855, lines 8, 7
the mint that never ceased: poem 486, lines 5–6
esoteric sips: poem 1452, lines 3–4
Every day life feels mightier: letter 298 (to Louise and Frances Norcross, 1864?)
I send two sunsets: poem 308

27   I reckon – when I count at all: poem 569, lines 1–8
A wounded deer – leaps highest: poem 165, line 1
Essential oils – are wrung: poem 675, lines 1–4
'Tis parching – vitalizes wine: poem 313, line 23

28   when I try to organize: letter 271 (to T. W. Higginson, 1862)
You must come down to Boston sometimes?: letter 330a (from T. W. Higginson, 1869)
Could it please your convenience; I do not cross: letter 330 (to T. W. Higginson, 1869)
to count the cats in Zanzibar: Thoreau, *Walden*, p. 322
the private sea: ibid., p. 321
Soto! Explore thyself! poem 832

29   Exultation is the going: poem 76
My own words so chill: letter 798 (to Joseph Chickering, 1883)
Who giants know: poem 796, lines 1–4
Alone, I cannot be: poem 298, lines 1–2
On my volcano grows the grass: poem 1677, line 1
Earthquake style: poem 601, line 5

30   had you looked in –: poem 296, lines 22–24
Dimity convictions: poem 401, line 5
On a columnar self: poem 789, line 1
The props assist the house: poem 1142
I remember her: MacGregor Jenkins, *Emily Dickinson, Friend and Neighbor* (Boston: Little,
   Brown and Co., 1930), pp. 30–33

32   She would stand looking down: Leyda II: 483
my words put all their feathers on: letter 190 (to Joseph Sweetser, 1858)
Admirabler show: poem 827, line 11
The birds jocoser sung: poem 794, line 10
Swerveless tune: poem 380, line 28
Perturbless plan: poem 724, line 10
How dare I, therefore: poem 766, lines 13–14
Without the snow's tableau: poem 285, lines 13–15

33   Inheritance, it is, to us: poem 321, lines 9–14
This is my letter to the world: poem 441, lines 1–4
I stepped from plank to plank: poem 875, lines 1–4
Come, sound his praise: *Pilgrim Hymnal* (Boston: Pilgrim Press, 1935), hymn 8

34   Just lost, when I was saved: poem 160, lines 1–6
uncontrolled, spasmodic: letter 265 (to T. W. Higginson, 1862)

35   Even so august a poet as Oliver Wendell Holmes: Mark A. DeWolfe Howe, *Memories of a
Hostess* [Mrs. James T. Fields] (Boston: Atlantic Monthly Press, 1922), p. 43
the only kangaroo: letter 268 (to T. W. Higginson, 1862)
He was trying to measure a cube: Johnson, *Complete Poems*, p. vi
That portion of the vision: poem 1126, line 9

Ned tells that the clock purrs: letter 315 (to Mrs. Holland, 1866)

On a strange mob: poem 1593, lines 9–17

36 Bring me the sunset in a cup: poem 128, line 1

in sovereign barns: poem 333, line 17

Baronial bees: poem 64, line 11

The wind . . . upholsterer: poem 602, lines 13, 16

The sunshine threw his hat away: poem 794, line 11

Death . . . His pallid furniture: poem 1230, lines 1, 3

Eternity's vast pocket, picked: poem 587, line 14

Summer folds her miracle: poem 342, lines 17–18

That whiffletree of amethyst: poem 1636, line 5

The auctioneer of parting: poem 1612, lines 1–4

If I read a book: Leyda II: 151 (quoted by T. W. Higginson, 1870)

rumor of delirium: poem 513, line 5

Death's tremendous nearness: poem 532, line 4

Purple ribaldry: poem 592, line 4

Edifice of ocean: poem 1217, line 9

confiscated Gods: poem 1260, line 40

The rat is the concisest tenant; Neither decree prohibit him: poem 1356, lines 1–2, 9–10

37 My faith that dark adores: poem 7, lines 22–24

Meanwhile – her wheeling king: poem 232, lines 8–10

receipted bliss: poem 1608, line 2

Codicil of doubt: poem 1012, line 3

Indemnity for loneliness: poem 1179, line 3

Acquitted – from that naked bar: poem 455, lines 15–16

the cube of the rainbow: poem 1484, line 1

Exponent of earth: poem 917, line 4

strata of iniquity: poem 1453, line 3

Enchantment's perihelion: poem 1299, line 5

Convex – and concave witness: poem 906, line 13

38 What respite from her thrilling toil: poem 1585, lines 5–8

Shall I take thee: poem 1126

I found a bird, this morning: letter 269 (to Dr. and Mrs. J. G. Holland, 1862?)

39 It is a cruel wrong: Leyda II: 430

letters and packages to Roswell Smith: Leyda II: 483

Glory is that bright tragic thing: poem 1660

40 So give me back to death: poem 1632, line 1

private, no flowers: Leyda II: 475

to Amherst to the funeral: Leyda II: 474–475

locked box in her sister's bedroom: Johnson, *Poems of Emily Dickinson*, I: xxxix

The beggar at the door for fame: poem 1240, line 1

41 She came to me with two day lilies: Leyda II: 151

Our log-rolling, our stumps and their politics: Ralph Waldo Emerson, "The Poet," *Complete Essays* (New York: Modern Library College Edition, 1950), p. 338

a great primitive poem: letter by Thoreau to H. G. O. Blake in *The Correspondence of Henry David Thoreau*, edited by Walter Harding and Carl Bode (New York: New York University Press, 1958), p. 445

genius in America: Emerson, "The Poet," p. 338

41   Come Muse migrate from Greece and Ionia: Walt Whitman, *Leaves of Grass*, edited by
Harold W. Blodgett and Sculley Bradley (New York: New York University Press, 1965),
p. 196

The ballots of eternity: poem 343, line 11

43   'Tis little I – could care for pearls: poem 466, lines 1–2

The breaking of the day: poem 155, lines 11–12

You'll know it – as you know 'tis noon: poem 420, lines 1–2

bulletins from immortality: cf. poem 827

the firmaments that fill her basket: cf. poem 352

the sea parts to show a further sea: cf. poem 695

A DICKINSON BIBLIOGRAPHY

Thomas H. Johnson, editor. *The Poems of Emily Dickinson (Including variant readings critically compared with all known manuscripts)*. Cambridge, Massachusetts: The Belknap Press of Harvard University Press, 1955. 3 vols.

This definitive edition of Emily Dickinson's poetry brings order to the confusion of manuscripts found after her death. The chronological arrangement of the poems and the choices among variants are the fruit of many years of Dickinson scholarship.

————. *The Complete Poems of Emily Dickinson*. Boston and Toronto: Little, Brown and Co., 1960.

This one-volume edition, published in both cloth and paperback, is handy for the general reader since it leaves out the variants and the commentary.

————. *Final Harvest*. Boston and Toronto: Little, Brown and Co., 1961.

Choosing among the seventeen hundred seventy-five poems and fragments in the complete edition, Johnson has here selected five hundred seventy-five.

————. *The Letters of Emily Dickinson*. Cambridge, Massachusetts: The Belknap Press of Harvard University Press, 1958. 3 vols.

"... You ask me to excuse the freedom of your letter Dear A. I think all things should be free with friends ..." (*Letters* I: 32). In this edition more than a thousand examples display the freedom, the candor, and the extreme sensitivity of a woman for whom letters were increasingly the only coinage of social exchange.

Jay Leyda. *The Years and Hours of Emily Dickinson*. New Haven: Yale University Press, 1960. 2 vols.

A chronology of thousands of short items drawn from newspapers, letters, sermons, town records, grocery lists, and many other primary sources forms the text of this fascinating "documentary biography." The first entry is the marriage intentions of Emily Dickinson's father and mother, recorded by the Amherst town clerk in 1828. The last is a letter about the poet's funeral in 1886. In their extraordinary detail these two volumes provide a vivid picture of Emily Dickinson's world.

Richard B. Sewall. *The Life of Emily Dickinson*. New York: Farrar, Straus and Giroux, 1974. 2 vols.

This wonderfully readable and exhaustive biography is both sensible and sensitive. One by one it examines the men and women who were crucial to Emily Dickinson. We see her reflected in the eyes of her friends and the members of her family, and we observe the poems springing from her life. As chapter succeeds patient chapter, a portrait of the poet emerges more and more clearly until she seems at last to stand in full light. The book is now available in an unabridged one-volume paperback.

FROM THE ARTIST'S NOTEBOOK

My paintings for this book were evoked primarily by Emily Dickinson's poetry and also by her letters, the atmosphere of her life in Amherst, and insights from many of the fine scholarly works about her art and life.

These paintings do not specifically illustrate a single poem, event, or poetic idea, but reflect these sources as well as shared feelings about life itself.

Many artists, among them Odilon Redon, have attempted to define the visual image which accompanies the word but does not merely serve it. We have terms like "harmonious contrast," "interpretation," "transmutation," or "visual metaphor." My term might be corroboration, or the term that Redon's friend Mellerio suggested, "parallélisme corrélatif."

In response to questions of technique, the paintings are on Strathmore 3-ply medium surface paper. I composed (from primary sources whenever possible) first in pencil. Using small Winsor Newton sable brushes and (for the first time) Winsor Newton watercolors instead of colored inks, I painted—erasing the pencil understructure as I progressed, building most tone with small interwoven lines. The only "white" is the infinity of light in the paper.

I invite the reader's participation in this book. It might be regarded not as a final entity but as a "working" book—a Dickinson Album. In the ample air we have provided around the selection of poems, you might wish to add other favorite Dickinson poems, aphorisms, phrases, as well as your own thoughts . . . press wildflowers . . . leaves . . . or letters!

To know Emily Dickinson's poetry and to know her life is a Gift of Light. These paintings are my grateful response.

Following are a few selections from my notebooks. The quotations from Emily Dickinson are given in italics.

Among the line drawings are these sources: the only photographic image of Emily Dickinson, with a snowdrop from the Homestead yard; Edward Dickinson's briefcase; utensils from the Homestead and from Austin Dickinson's home, the Evergreens; E.D.'s gathering of a snail, acorn, etc., for Susan Gilbert; E.D.'s hourglass, thought to have been given her by Bowles or Higginson; the keyhole of her bedroom door; the French microscope, dated 1860, owned by Edward Hitchcock, Sr., geologist and president of Amherst College.

"FLOOD SUBJECT"
title page   diameter 9 inches   23 cm.
Mandala for Emily · *Centre* and *Circumference* · circumference—ever-expanding but finite, like universe—end of definition, beginning of unknown · *Molten Blue* · my peonies (Festiva Maxima) flecks of red · flame · sea rhythms · fins, feathers, wind · centrifuge · *Wheel of Cloud* · *Immortality . . . is the Flood Subject* · E.D. mentions peony in letter · *the recollecting of Bloom* · *Of an inland soul to sea* · hymn "So fades a summer cloud away"

CARLO DREAMS

page 53   12⅛ x 10⅞ inches   31 x 27.5 cm.

E.D.'s father buys her a brown Newfoundland · *Tell Carlo— | He'll tell me!* · Melville, Byron owned Newfoundlands · E.D.'s sea imagery—Newfoundlands shown performing rescues at sea in paintings and in children's magazines of the 1800s · India shawl on E.D.'s sleigh bed · Vinnie's plaid shawl and watchful cat (E.D. disliked cats —among Vinnie's cats Tabby, Drummy Doodles, Buffy Tootsie) · In 1876, E.D. to Thomas Wentworth Higginson: *Carlo died . . . Would you instruct me now?*

"EAST"

page 67   14 x 10½ inches   35.5 x 26.5 cm.

July—a Friday night in 1858—*strange blooms arise on many stalks* · E.D.'s bedroom door reversed to open toward the *East* and Pelham Hills · *the door to eternity is hinged open* · *Then reversed the Door* · *heliotrope by the apron's full–the mountain colored one* · *an astral wake* · constellation to east over Pelham Hills—Pegasus · E.D. called Austin *Brother Pegasus* · infinity of light beyond the scrim of dark · dark stars in heliotrope flowers · *do you dwell in the East?* · *Night is the morning's Canvas*

EARTHLIGHT

page 81   15 x 12 inches   38 x 30.5 cm.

two Legacies · *Calvary* · *Home* · *Until the Realm of you* · *Scarlet Experiment!* · earthlight · *A tender–thoughtful Moon* · *the new Coat–that the Tailor made* based on coat worn by Samuel Bowles in photograph · *At Centre of the Sea* · *Meridian* and *Midnight* · *My Blue Peninsula* · a black maelstrom or void—contrary to E.D.'s concept of a light infinity

A LANDSCAPE SO LONE

page 95   10⅛ x 9¼ inches   25.5 x 23.5 cm.

November 27, 1854, E.D. to Susan Gilbert: *and the scene should be—solitude, and the figures—solitude—and the lights and shades, each a solitude. I could fill a chamber with landscapes so lone* · *seldoms of the mind* · *That polar privacy* · George Eliot, *Middlemarch*: "on the other side of silence" · E.D. colors—browns, blues, and white · cup and saucer of Dickinson gold and white china on E.D.'s cherry writing table · reflection · Higginson's remark to E.D.: "that fine edge of thought"

OF STIR AND PLACE

page 109   14⅜ x 11⅞ inches   36.5 x 30 cm.

Friday I tasted Life. It was a vast morsel. A circus passed the house—still I feel the red in my mind · *Slow tramp the Centuries, | And the Cycles wheel!* · *The fine–unvarying Axis | That regulates the Wheel* · when a circus arrived by rail, the early morning procession traveled west on Main Street past the Homestead · the Homestead, a brown-yellow, reflected in cage wagon mirror · trees believed to be horse chestnuts · a cage wagon called the "Whiskers Wagon" · *the miles of Stare* in carved figures on succession of tableau and cage wagons · *Civilization–spurns–the Leopard! | . . . Pity–the Pard–that left her Asia–*

"MUCH BOUQUET"

page 123   12 x 9⅛ inches   30.5 x 23 cm.

Clara Newman, a cousin who lived at the Evergreens, tells of incident when E.D.'s nephew Ned (around 1865? 1870?) left high-top rubber boots at Homestead. E.D. returned them "erect and spotless" on a silver tray, their tops running over with her flowers · E.D. to Ned: *And ever be sure of me, Lad* · *Nature–the Gentlest Mother is,* / *Impatient of no Child* · table by Homestead kitchen window overlooking lawn · grass unmowed, pear tree still exists · a silver tray owned by Dickinson family · kitchen *apple green* with "deep yellow" casings (chip reveals a brown yellow) · E.D. worked a bookmark—an arrow with a wreath around it—knife · E.D. included poems with gifts of flowers · *"Unto the little, unto me"*

"IMAGE OF LIGHT"
page 137   10¾ x 9¾ inches   27.5 x 24.5 cm.
E.D.'s white dress · Jane Langton notes large pocket unusual in dress of day · poem on E.D.'s stationery—she often wrote drafts on odd assortment of envelopes, shopping lists, backs of recipes, etc. · *Domains in my Pocket* · *Indies in the hand*

"SWEET VELOCITY"
page 147   15½ x 12 inches   39.5 x 30.5 cm.
E.D.'s nephew Gilbert died on October 5, 1883 · obituary described Gib as townspeople saw him, riding his velocipede · a fragile *Chariot* riderless · *thy Rendezvous of Light* · *Oh for a Disc to the Distance* · *Auroral light* · this is Gilbert Dickinson's velocipede. I doubt any other has ridden it in nearly one hundred years · front wheel turned to the distance and to the light · a charmed object

PROGRESSION
page 153   11¼ x 8¼ inches   28.5 x 21 cm.
May 15, 1886—E.D. "ceases to breathe" · *Little Cousins–called back* · *The Bodiless–begun* · funeral on May 19 · flowers present included bluets (Innocence), violets, wild geraniums, pansies, liles of the valley, buttercups, one pink cypripedium, ferns, and groundpine · succession · E.D. on May 16, 1848: *I love spring and spring flowers* · wildflowers her favorite, then gardenias and Daphne Odora · *The immortality of Flowers must enrich our own* · *Oh, Matchless Earth* · *Forever–is composed of Nows* · *Jubilee and Knell* · *we are permanent temporarily* · MacGregor Jenkins remembered E.D. standing on "rug" (blanket) spread on grass, working in garden · Dickinson blanket—red and black · white dress · "warm hair" · *my Hair is bold, like the Chestnut bur* · Mattie describes E.D.—medium height, decisive manner, dark expressive eyes, Titian hair, white skin, low-pitched soft voice, wore cameo pin · cadence · the poet as prism · *a Columnar Self–* Helen Hunt to E.D., March 1876: "You are a great poet."

ACKNOWLEDGMENTS

My appreciation and thanks to Mrs. Kendall B. DeBevoise, who lives at the Homestead; to her neighbor and friend, Mary Landis Hampson at the Evergreens; and to "my trusty Jane—my friend encourager, and sincere counciller," for their important contributions to this book.

Also, my thanks to the following persons and institutions: Lorrie Otto, "Preceptress" of wildflowers; Robert Parkinson, Research Center Director, Circus World Museum and Library, Baraboo, Wisconsin; Chris Rowe, Manfred Olson Planetarium, University of Wisconsin, Milwaukee; Department of Astronomy, Amherst College; Rae Ann Nager and resources in the Dickinson Room, Houghton Library, Harvard University; the Milwaukee Zoo, Milwaukee, Wisconsin; Bob and Jean Quandt, owners of the brown Newfoundland Edenglen's Brown Sugar; John Lancaster, Special Collections Librarian-Archivist, the Robert Frost Library, Amherst College; William A. Mueller, Director, Physical Plant, Amherst College; the Emily Dickinson Room, Jones Library, Amherst, Massachusetts; Mrs. Kate Hanke, Amherst, Massachusetts; Karen Hitchcock, East Orleans, Massachusetts; Alice Pickman, Lincoln, Massachusetts; the Milwaukee Public Museum and members of the staff; Martha Dickinson Bianchi, for recollections in her book *Emily Dickinson Face to Face*; the late W. G. Reynolds of Tuscaloosa, Alabama; the New York Public Library, General Research and Humanities Division.

Nancy Ekholm Burkert

Several people helped this book along by correcting my text: X. J. Kennedy, Richard Sewall, Mrs. Kendall B. DeBevoise, and Mrs. Kate Hanke. Ralph Franklin provided indispensable editorial advice.

Nancy Burkert and I are grateful to book designer Lance Hidy, and to those at New York Graphic Society who worked on *Acts of Light*: editor-in-chief Floyd Yearout, Susan Feldman, Betsy Pitha, Nan Jernigan, Janet Swan, and, most especially, editor Robin Bledsoe.

Jane Langton

INDEX OF FIRST LINES

12